write free

jennifer probst

This is a work of fiction. Names, characters, organizations, places, events, and incidents are either products of the author's imagination or are used fictitiously.

Text copyright © 2025 by Triple J Publishing Inc.

ISBN: e-book: 979-8-9909913-4-7

ISBN: print: 979-8-9909913-3-0

All rights reserved.

No part of this book may be reproduced, or stored in a retrieval system, or transmitted in any form or by any means, electronic, mechanical, photocopying, recording, or otherwise, without express written permission of the publisher.

Cover design by Lauren Layne

Introduction

In a world of less attention, short videos, scrolling, and AI, writers are always looking to write more, grow faster, and market savvier. But what if what we needed instead was bite-size pieces of quiet inspiration? A way to feel re-connected to our Muse, creativity, joy, and other writers? To feel not so alone and allow a reset?

In *Write Free*, Jennifer Probst has put together a book of essays about writing. Ranging from laugh-out loud stories about comparing writing and orgasms; to heartful advice on how to get through struggles of block and grief, *Write Free* allow creatives to take a breath, a laugh; a smile; and remind themselves why they write.

Introduction

Easy to read and re-connect with our cranky Muse, so we can get back to what we were born to do.

Share our stories.

Praise for Jennifer Probst

"There's a reason Probst is the gold-standard in contemporary romance." —Lauren Layne, New York Times bestselling author

"Jennifer Probst knows how to bring the swoons and the sexy!" —Amy Reichert, author of The Coincidence of Coconut Cake

"For a sexy, fun-filled warmhearted read, look no further than Jennifer Probst!" —Jill Shalvis, New York Times bestselling author

"Probst is one of the best contemporary romance authors I know!" —Angela Carr, Under the Covers blog

Praise for *Write Naked*: A Bestseller's Secrets to Writing Romance & Navigating the Path to Success:

"With wit and humor and heart-wrenching honesty, Jennifer Probst pens a winner with *Write Naked*, a book for all writers—from the aspirant just sitting down at the keyboard to the multi-published, best-selling author dominating the shelves. *Write Naked* has a place of prominence on my keeper shelf." —J. Kenner, New York Times bestselling author

"Authenticity is the core ingredient of every successful book, and to bring forth the type of raw honesty readers connect to, writers must get naked, placing their own beating heart on the page. Using incredible insight and finesse, Jennifer Probst shows writers how to do this, sharing many valuable lessons from her impressive career along the way. An inspiring read for writers of all levels." —Angela Ackerman, bestselling author of The Emotion Thesaurus: A Writer's Guide to Character Expression

"Jennifer Probst brings something magical to her writing, and with *Write Naked* she gives you insight into her process. The most important thing a writer can do is hone their process, and this book is a valuable tool to use in doing that. Highly recommend!" —Bob Mayer, New York Times bestselling author

"*Write Naked* is a book all 'newbie' and seasoned writers need in their life." —Jennifer L. Armentrout, #1 New York Time bestselling author

"A must read! Jennifer's *Write Naked* is refreshingly honest, insightful, and a real pleasure to read and feel inspired by. A true gem!" —Katy Evans, New York Times bestselling author

"Funny, truthful, and entertaining—*Write Naked* is a book all writers need in their life!" —Melissa Foster, New York Times bestselling author

"*Write Naked* is perfect for individuals considering entering the writing field or well-seasoned authors! Wherever you are in your writing journey...this book is for you." —Audrey Carlan, #1 New York Times bestselling author

Other Books by Jennifer Probst

Nonfiction

Write Naked: A Bestseller's Secrets to Writing Romance & Navigating the Path to Success

Write True: A Bestseller's Guide to Writing Craft & Achieving Success in the Romance Industry

Writers Inspiring Writers: What I Wish I'd Known

The Outer Banks Series

Book of the Month

The Reluctant Flirt

Meet Me in Italy Series

Our Italian Summer

The Secret Love Letters of Olivia Moretti

A Wedding in Lake Como

To Sicily with Love

The Red Series

Yearn

Crave

Covet

The Twist of Fate Series
Meant to Be
So It Goes
Save the Best for Last

The Sunshine Sisters Series
Love on Beach Avenue
Temptation on Ocean Drive
Forever in Cape May
Christmas in Cape May

The Stay Series
The Start of Something Good
A Brand New Ending
All Roads Lead to You
Something Just Like This
Begin Again

The Billionaire Builders Series
Everywhere and Every Way
Any Time, Any Place
Somehow, Some Way

All or Nothing at All

The Searching For ... Series
Searching for Someday
Searching for Perfect
Searching for Beautiful
Searching for Always
Searching for You
Searching for Mine
Searching for Disaster

The Marriage to a Billionaire Series
The Marriage Bargain
The Marriage Trap
The Marriage Mistake
The Marriage Merger
The Book of Spells
The Marriage Arrangement

The Steele Brothers Series
Catch Me
Play Me
Dare Me
Beg Me

Reveal Me

Sex on the Beach Series
Beyond Me
Chasing Me

The Hot in the Hamptons Series
Summer Sins

Stand-Alone Novels
Dante's Fire
Executive Seduction
All the Way
The Holiday Hoax
The Grinch of Starlight Bend
The Charm of You

Author's Note

I grew up reading endless books about writing.

I was not only hungry for knowledge on craft, but enthralled by reading about other authors' lives. I wanted to know how they lived; how they wrote; what they thought; and chased every piece of advice possible so I could fill my creative well.

Along the way, as I learned more and more, I found myself re-reading many books that broke up chapters into short essays or reflections. I loved being able to get a hit and then go on with my day. Some of these treasured, well-worn books on my shelf are *On Writing* by Stephen King; *Writing Down the Bones* by Natalie Goldberg; *Still Writing* by Dani Shapiro; and *Bird by Bird* by Anne

Lamott. I re-read Michael Ventura's polarizing piece, *The Talent of the Room* regularly. *The War of Art* by Stephen Pressfield is an old friend quietly reminding me to step into my Resistance and move through.

With my fourth writing book, my goal was simple: gather up years of posts, articles, and essays I've penned over the years and compile them into one book. It's important to listen to our younger selves—that person was a different type of writer. We are always evolving just as we are always aging. I smiled a lot when I re-visited some of my beliefs on writing, my struggles as a new writer, and became amazed at my younger wisdom wrapped up in big dreams.

Write Free contains my perspective on a long writing career in bite-sized pieces. Many were previously posted on my website blog, or Substack, or were published as guest articles. I also included new essays that touch on marketing, branding, publicity, and pivoting during challenging moments.

This book is a journey. Stop along the way to pause, reflect, and think about your own writing. There are questions posed at the end of many essays and I invite you to reflect deeper on them.

This creative gift is a living, breathing thing. It deserves our attention. And it's bigger than chasing the money or the fame or the fleeting praise from readers, publishers, and other authors.

It's also a map of my own personal journey; an intimate look at not only my work, but my family, my struggles, and a peek into my daily life. I tried to leave most of my original work as is, only smoothing out the jagged parts, because my younger voice is important. I wanted to respect her.

Writing is done alone in a room, yet the goal is to share your work with the world. This type of delicate balance needs care and nurturing. Reading about others on the journey can heal and restore our faith; to remind ourselves we are okay.

We are simply writers trying to tell our story in the best way we can.

I hope this book makes you braver, freer, and more at peace with your own voice.

May the words be with you.

Chapter One

Writing and Orgasms

WRITING a book is like experiencing an orgasm.

Ah. Did I get your attention?

Let me explain further before everyone quits their current job to become a writer.

1. The Hook

The delicious sense of sexual tension is almost as good as a climax. Almost. Anticipation settles like a misty cloud, slowly taking over our senses, driving us forward. It's sweet, and slow, and fulfilling. It promises the world, and wraps us in a haze of longing. We fall under its spell and siren's promise of pure pleasure.

When I begin a book, I usually know how I want to hook readers. Writing those first few chapters usually entrance me. I'm looking forward to the journey of learning new characters. There are no issues to deal with in the beginning, just a happy getting-to-know-you phase with all the good and none of the bad. I feel as if the world is mine for the taking. I feel powerful and creative and strong. I throw myself into the deep end and savor every word on the page that lead to more…and more. I am Rocky. I am the seduced. I cannot wait to see what happens next.

2. The Sagging Middle

This is where the speed bumps happen. And yes, it happens with sex, too. A touch or a move that doesn't please you. The sudden worry you won't be able to cross the finish line. The reminder to stop thinking and just feel; be in the moment; flow with the ups and downs; the good and bad within the journey. This is the delicate part where you can shut down, quit, or hold back.

This is where the brain comes in and tries to wrestle control from the body. *Do I look fat in this position? Did I make a weird noise? Do they like what I'm doing?*

The middle is where the doubts rush in. If we can just relax and let go; trust the story and our instinct; we sense it will all work out.

3. The End

Suddenly, we're grooving again. Moving forward with each delicious step toward a fulfillment we've dreamed about since the beginning of the encounter. Our bodies shake with excitement. God, it's right there! So close…the tension is ready to explode with one last touch--

When writing, I rarely sleep toward the end of my book, my mind full of character chatter and the motivation to keep writing, go faster, go deeper, but once again it's my body and Muse that need to take over. My fingers fly, I chase the story in a fit of building pleasure and anticipation until I reach the sweetest two words in history.

The End.

The Climax.

The Orgasm.

. . .

God, was that as good for you as it was for me?

Here's something else I learned from writing.

It's all about the journey. Too many straight orgasms without the lovely swells of good and bad, up and down, gentle to hard, would be…too much.

Maybe we'd stop appreciating the goal. Each step in the journey is precious, so next time you find yourself at any of the phases, take a deep breath and surrender. Glide toward the end and trust you'll get there, especially if you let go and turn off that asshole brain of ours.

It'll be worth it.

Chapter Two

Writing and The Way You Handle the Waves

I TOOK A VACATION LAST WEEK. An overdue one. I met up with my big Italian family and headed to Puerto Rico for some sun. I have that horrible winter seasonal disorder so I struggle, and a bit of sun and beach always heals me in all the right ways.

We had seven children with us, which made it even more chaotic and fun, and my cheeks and stomach hurt from smiling nonstop.

We had the pleasure of being able to visit Flamenco beach, which was rated number 3 in the entire world. Pretty cool, huh? Like all things worth doing, the trip took effort and time. Someone had to get up at six am and get on line to buy tickets for the ferry, then had to wait in that line till 9am when people actually began showing up. The ferry ride was an hour, and when we got to the small island, we rented Jeeps.

We stood in blistering heat, eating melty ice cream, while we waited for the Jeeps to be delivered. It took us a while to get to the beach because most of the narrow roads were blocked, and we ended up backing up and praying nonstop for survival while we negotiated between honking trunks and confused construction workers.

But once we arrived there, we feasted on paradise.

Turquoise waters. Powdery bleached-white sand that stretched out in unspoiled glory. The mountains shimmered in the distance as if looking over its ward, making sure all was well. The waves were just big enough to have fun, but if you got pulled under, there was no undertow like the Long Island and New Jersey beaches I'm used to.

We all jumped into the water. I soaked in the sun and watched the children play. Then noticed something important.

They all had different techniques for dealing with the waves.

Write Free

The two girls were fearless—they went out as far as possible and took on each crest with an aggressive intent to beat Mother Nature. When they got dragged under, they got right back up, teeth gritted; determined to wrest victory from the next one.

My oldest son liked the middle. He didn't go too far out, nor be too far back. He analyzed each wave to decide how he'd attack it. If a wave was too big, he'd dive under instead of running away. If it was manageable, he chose to try and ride it to shore. The mini ones he just jumped over like a little duck and got wet.

My youngest son stayed far, far back. He watched his cousins with puzzlement, as if wondering why they'd try to take on the ocean and think they'd win. Tentatively walking a few steps, gaze focused on each swell, he'd quickly run back to safety and then jump them on his own terms. It was obvious he thought the others were not that intelligent.

My other niece liked to dive. Didn't matter if they were big, medium, or small. Each obstacle was an opportunity for her to go deep and take a risk. Many times, she was battered and dragged over the sand but it didn't stop her. She'd smile at each of her victories, smugly believing she was the ultimate victor against the ocean. Even if my youngest didn't believe it.

As always, my mind went to my writing, like it does for every analogy of life. I am currently in the midst of writing a book and searching for the loose threads of the story, trying to pull them through and figure out the deepest levels of my characters to make them real.

I was struck by a fascinating realization. Each part of every book I write imitates a child's unique plan on taking on the ocean.

In the beginning, I am fearless. I wade deep, sure I've got this book nailed, full of superhuman ego that zaps in my veins like fire. God, I love that part. It's too fleeting, and disappears way too quickly to be replaced with....

The first quarter. This is the time in my book I've slowed down, and am studying the map of where I'm going. Did I make a wrong turn? Should I dive quicker, back off, or just let the mini waves carry me to shore? I don't mind this part as much because the next phase is the worst for me...

The middle. I hate the middle. I become my youngest, trapped in a story I can't really figure out and refusing to take a step further. I make a bit of progress here and there, maybe one scene goes well for a while but then the wave crests and I need to run back quickly before I get pummeled. It is a time I'm testing my story, deciding where it's leading, and not sure yet whether I can trust my instincts.

But then, oh, then, I get to dive. I pass the middle and see the final stretch ahead of me, and there is no fear left. I know what I'm doing again, and I'll go back and fix the rest of the crap later. This is the time I dive under every wave and come up smiling, not noticing anything but how good it feels. I am one with nature. I am one with the book.

Every aspect of life can relate back to writing.

Where are you in your writing journey right now? Is there a life experience you can note down that reminds you of writing?

Chapter Three

The Invisible Tools in Writing

I was talking to my son tonight at the dinner table, explaining a part of my book I was working on.

Well, to be honest, the first ten minutes was me whining about how badly it was going, how my Muse is being all sorts of stubborn and mean girl, and how this was a terrible, stressful job sometimes.

My son said he couldn't imagine anything better than being able to wake up and write a book and get paid for it. He said I have the best job in the entire world.

That statement got me a bit teary eyed and reset my crankiness. After that part of the discussion/ranting ended, we got to the learning portion of our dinner.

My son has recently instituted the topic of What Did You Learn Today? We go around the table and everyone shares one thing they learned from their day.

This is harder to do when you're not in school stuffing facts and figures and interesting tidbits into the brain. I get excited when I have to google something for my story or do research because I know I'm clear for the night. And when things get bad, we throw out stuff like: I learned Dad is the one to always eat the last brownie, and then my youngest son judges if it truly counts as a fact learned or we're just trying to pull one over on them.

Back to the writing.

I was writing *So It Goes* and during one of my scenes, I needed something to show the heroine a softer side to my hero. Since he's a billionaire, my heroine noticed his luxurious office held an impressive book shelf with tons of books. Many contained rare editions.

She immediately assumed the books were for show and he hadn't read any of them. At the end of the meeting, in an effort to get close to her, my hero said she could ask any question she wanted and he'd answer truthfully.

Her question, of course, was if he'd actually read any of those books and if so, how many?

My hero said yes, he'd read them all, and they were his best friends as he grew up. He went to the shelf and pulled out *Slaughterhouse Five* by Kurt Vonnegut, citing it as his favorite book and author.

Then my hero quotes the line, So it Goes, which loops back to my title.

When I began researching the term So it Goes, I was brought immediately to Vonnegut and his work. I read about the power of the phrase in his writing, and what he hoped to accomplish in Slaughterhouse Five.

My son's favorite author is Vonnegut. He adored *Slaughterhouse Five* and when I mentioned this part to of my scene to him, my son lit up.

He confirmed that line was used each time something died – whether it was a person or a car battery. It was a brutal form of acceptance explored within the book. Since I've never read it

(I know!), I enjoyed getting to know my son's opinions and analysis. Within our discussion, I began to unearth a bit of Vonnegut treasure.

This conversation was a teachable moment for me.

My writing is built on connectedness. I took the Clifton Strengths test and received coaching from Becca Syme in her Write Faster Academy. The goal of learning your top ten strengths is an important part of accepting how you write and how you approach your writing life.

With connectedness being number 6, I know it's an important strength to lean into with my writing. For me, every element of life is a connection, like a spiderweb bound together with a delicate, yet strong foundation. From the title, theme, and what I want the characters to evolve from, I try to place markers throughout the story that I can weave through to make it a fuller experience for a reader.

This is a building block of craft that's sometimes hard for me to explain. It's like smoke – invisible but always there. Weaving all these elements together is critical for me to make sense of the story and write the best book possible. I couldn't have worked on this element years ago. I was too busy working on more solid things such as setting, active voice, and GMC (goal, motivation, conflict).

But as I grow as a writer reaching fifty books, I can more clearly see both my process and my goal.

Theme is an important part of my story's structure. I always choose a theme for the overall story ARC and my individual character's ARC. Fleshing out both makes my books richer.

The craft is done in the background and shouldn't be visible on the page unless you are specifically looking for it. Teaching beginning writers theme and connectedness is difficult, because I believe there's a hierarchy of craft that needs to be transitioned through first. Newer writers need to focus on baser craft techniques, master them, and then the higher levels can be better understood.

And that's okay. It took me a long time to reach that type of craft mastery and I still desperately need editing.

It's another gift of this business—the constant learning of craft and process. The struggle of the blank page can be bad but it can also be the most exciting part of our lives. We always get to start over and recreate.

What other person gets to do that in their job?

My son was right. We both taught each other something that night.

Can I use that as my learning tool for tomorrow's dinner?

Chapter Four

A Day in Deadline Hell

30 DAYS UNTIL DEADLINE.

Gotta get my shit together.

I look at my calendar and ruthlessly scrub everything I can from it. I will write night and day. 3K minimum. No excuses, no whining, no time left for my intellection to ponder or my connectedness to try and think of ways to blend the theme together with the ARCS of the characters. I need raw words on the page.

Kids off to school. Gotta answer email. Crap, I forgot I have those copyedits and those FB ads I was supposed to schedule. Kohls credit card is due already? I'll just pay that and move on to the rest later.

Write Free

I set up my headphones and playlist. Are you kidding me? My headphones are dead – I forgot to charge them. I'll have to listen on speaker while they charge up.

My manuscript is open on my screen. I read the last few paragraphs. Ugh, what happens next? Why are there endless scenes of them in the conference room and diner? Is that all I can write about? I'm so bored…

I write a few hundred words. My mother calls. I pick up eagerly.

Half hour later. Oh, I forgot that podcast I need to promo on social media. I'll do that, then back to work. Also, more coffee. Oh, dogs need to go out.

Good, I'm back. Where was I? In the conference room again? Ugh, they have to have sex soon because I don't know what to write next. They're not even close to sex. Can I speed things up?

I write 1K.

Yes, I'm on the move! Who cares if they've eaten more pancakes—they're talking and bantering. Banter is good. I need to stretch and eat lunch. I deserve a little break, right? Then I'll write like the wind all afternoon. Ugh, that was an awful cliché.

Oh, a new Real Housewives episode dropped! I'll watch for a bit, eat, then back at it.

Two hours later.

Shit! What happened? OMG I'll make more coffee – no, I'm supposed to be drinking more water for my diet, I'll open up some seltzer. Dogs again?

Fifteen minutes later.

Back to it. Headphones are charged at least. Why does my editor need this book so early? The release isn't till February. I'll do it later. I do better under pressure, anyway. But I told myself I'd get ahead this time so better to dive back into the story while it's fresh in my mind.

Half hour later. Okay, I got this. I am a goddess. I've written New York Times bestsellers. This is my forty something book. I know how to write! Why is the GMC so weak, though? I'll worry about that in edits. Right now I need WORDS. At least, 1700 more to keep to my deadline.

This book sucks. I hate this book. I was so stupid to believe it was a good idea at the time.

500 words more. I need to check Facebook real quick. Super quick. Hey, that looks like a good book to read—I should buy it. It's craft and will

help me out. OMG, reverse harem is on sale? Click on that, baby. Where did those shoes come from? Do I need more shoes? No. But maybe I do? Let me just check.

One hour, two books, and two pairs of shoes later.

Are you kidding me? I have to get to work, no more messing around! The dogs AGAIN? More water. Better music. Ugh, I hate this book. Can they have sex yet?

500 words.

Are the boys home yet? You gotta be kidding me—I'm so tired.

Much later…

Dinner? Yes! I'm ready!

I finish and realize I still have to write 1K. I may die. This book sucks. But I can't watch Big Brother with my family until my word count is done.

And I forgot to meditate today. I didn't walk either. Maybe I'll dance around the office for a few minutes to loosen up? I like this song…

I sit my ass back down. Where was I? Banter. Sexual tension. Why do I keep writing about this secondary character? Do I care? Will a reader care?

There's no description—it's like the entire book is taking place in a white, windless tunnel. My editor is going to kill me.

Focus. Write.

500 words later.

I'm going to die. I'll write 3500 tomorrow and make up for it. I'll do anything to get away from this book. Isn't it supposed to be better by the halfway mark? I'm only writing 70K this time—I can't manage 90K.

I'm done with those longer type books. Maybe I'll even write 65K. My editor will just have to deal with it. But if they haven't had sex yet, I need to squeeze in extra chapters or the emotion won't be grounded.

I hate my life.

I shut down the computer and leave.

I watch Big Brother. Read. Snack. Hang with kids. Stay up way too late.

REPEAT.

I cannot wait until this book is done.

Chapter Five

What I Learned as a Writer Watching Project Runway

I'M A REALITY TELEVISION WHORE.

I don't even care I'm telling you either. Yes, I'm highly educated. A feminist. An artist. But there's just something about reality television that allows my consistently churning mind to turn off for a little bit, kick back with a glass of wine, and relax. This type of entertainment is a candy coated, sugary, delicious sweet for my brain. I'm swept away and when I come back, I feel better.

One of my favorite reality shows is Project Runway. Of course, I adore fashion, so besides gawking at the amazing stylish art that is created in a record time limit, I'm amazed at the creative process each of the designers deals with.

At one of the All Stars, three designers created eight looks to make a complete collection. They did it in four days.

I've written a novella in a three-day weekend. Personally, I've visited this hell before and it ain't pretty. Watching the designers struggle to transition their sketches to reality reminded me of when I have a story so well thought out in my brain, I wish to God I could just tell it to the bookstores rather than actually write it. Because too many times when I commit the words to paper, it's not what I originally wanted or dreamed of. It's different. I either have to work with the skeleton I've sketched out on paper, tweak my original idea, or make it something else I hadn't planned on.

Each designer had a unique design process. One sketched different parts first, then pieced together the outfit. One liked to create a bit from each outfit and work on them simultaneously. Another needed to complete one at a time in an orderly fashion.

Two designers seemed to embrace their processes wholly and utterly—owning their vision and execution with a determination that came from practice and time and sheer stubbornness. Both of them had done the show before and made it to the finale. Both were back to prove to themselves they could do win.

The third designer seemed to struggle with his creative process a bit more. He'd grown leaps and bounds from his past season, but once he gave up and surrendered to the negative, devilish, whispery thoughts in his head that said he'd lose because his outfit sucked. I listened to his rant asking why the hell was he going through this crap anyway? He could go home and be happy and leave it all behind because it meant nothing anyway. Right? Right?

He walked away. But he came back. He had no choice because design was the driving force of his soul, and it was time he just accepted it and give in and give up.

He did. He finished a gorgeous collection. He proved what could be done, and learned the win wasn't necessarily the prize money—like publication, and endless followers, and a movie deal, and fame.

It was about his collection and how he loved what he put out into the world.

Some of the judges loved his work and were very encouraging. One was extremely harsh and a tad cruel. She called herself honest, but I winced when she uttered some of her comments. You could tell he wanted to argue and defend. You could also tell when he accepted her words with a nod of the head and thank you, but his eyes told a different story. His eyes gleamed with his own rebellion, because deep down, he loved what he had done, and if he had to do it over, he'd do the same damn thing.

That's power.

What did all this remind me?

Besides to dress better and somehow get invited to one of those cool fashion shows, it reminded me it's about the book. The art. The product.

The win is wonderful. We go for the win, and there's nothing wrong with it. But the real win is what we have created through our determination and blood and sweat and tears. When the new release erupts into the world, and butterflies take flight in my stomach, and fear of the unknown assaults me from all angles, I go back to the book.

Did I do the best I could? Did I write a great

story? Did I do everything in my power to make it great and try to reach readers?

If it's a yes, then I did my job. I can sleep at night. I can be proud of my art.

Next stop?

Project Runway?

Sigh. No, then I'd have to go put on shoes…

Chapter Six

Writing Truths on Release Day

It's my release day.

My book, *Everywhere and Every Way*, is live everywhere – and the start of a brand new HGTV inspired romance series.

It's so very hard to try and express how a writer feels when her book goes live. I compare it to watching one of your children go out in the world and be their own person. You may have birthed them, but they belong to themselves.

Same as a book. From creation and birth, to the hard teen years of the sagging middle, to endless revisions to make sure they can live and thrive on their own, this book has a special place because it's the beginning of a brand new world.

Diving into a new series is scary and exhilarating. I want everyone to love the book as much as I did.

I also know everyone can't. That would just be...weird. Like living in a Stepford world where nothing goes wrong.

NYT Bestselling Author Bob Mayer once told me this: "Once the book is published, it no longer belongs to you. It belongs to the world."

He's right. I can only watch from afar and hope my book is loved. I feel like I worked as hard as I possibly could, and regret nothing.

Still, I haven't slept in two days, and my stomach feels like I'm ready to take a final in high school!

And that is why writing also takes a leap of faith. Like motherhood. Or anything else really beautiful and worthy in this life. So, I'm stepping back, concentrating on the new book I'm currently birthing, and need to trust whatever happens it will all be okay.

I've come a long way from the girl who'd scribble essays into her notebook and give them with a rapidly pounding heart to my Mom to read. Stories eventually need readers. Readers give them life and purpose.

But to get to that point, we need to take scary leaps and share. Put ourselves out there to get rejected, mocked, or not taken seriously. Read chapters to critique partners; send to editors and beta readers; and go online to market so readers will find us.

Sometimes, that one release day is a build up of years of work. Careful set up to promote and get as many people as possible to look at our baby; to like it; to buy it; to love it; to read it.

Yet, once we release it to the world, we are no longer in control. Sure, we can tweak blurbs and keywords, to do sales and TikTok videos and a million other ways to build up our foundation.

But the story is done. That chapter is written.

Release day is a time to breathe and remind yourself it will all be okay, no matter what happens with your book. A time for reflection and kindness. A time to celebrate what you were brave enough to accomplish.

Happy Release Day to all my fellow authors. It's going to be a great day.

Chapter Seven

Refilling the Well

The creative life is hard, yet fulfilling.

My writing changed when I began treating it as a business rather than a hobby. This meant giving myself deadlines, not quitting on a book that I felt wasn't working, brainstorming for series that could build with my readers, and non-stop deadlines.

To be honest, sometimes I reached a point of burnout. I remember confessing the book I was working on was really hard, and that I had lost a lot of my joy in the creation phase because I was consistently worried about writing faster and keeping to deadline. Projects were already laid out in front of me for over a year. Maybe more. I had little wiggle room.

Or so I thought.

It's taken me some time, but I'm finally starting to understand it's critical to have some down time in between projects. This past year, I finished a 100+K book, and in ten days a novella was due. And not a short novella. No, this one was going to be about 40K or more.

I panicked.

Not only over deadline, but that I'd have no creative juice left to pour into my next book. There was no way I intended to distribute a crappy book. I was ready to pull it if I couldn't make it work and damn the consequences.

I had a small blessing in the arrival of my Muse. She was so excited about the novella, the story streamed from me like no other before, and I basically wrote the book in ten days, though I had extended the deadline. It was sheer poetry and damn was I grateful.

Sometimes my bitchy Muse doesn't show up at all, let alone when I desperately need her!

I now have some down time before I need to dive into another massive book. My other two projects are small and can be done in increments to free up some time this summer. I've had the past two weeks off from serious writing, only having to do promotion for my new novel and all the business matters that come from being an author, but as the days drifted by, I began to relax and do things I haven't done in forever.

I cook now. I really enjoy it. Since I've been on a diet and lost weight, I can't rely on the pizza, Chinese and numerous restaurants that have made up my life. Instead, I experimented with wholesome recipes and found an exciting new world opening up to me.

Kale chips. Organic fruit smoothies. Garlic mashed cauliflower. Homemade hummus and salsa and tomato sauce that used to be bought from containers. It's become an adventure, where I blast my music, dance in my kitchen, and cook.

When I'm working seriously on a book, I don't have the time. I rely on my husband and he does a great job, but it's nice to finally be the one to put dinner on the table and try recipes that are healthy. Kind of like a new chapter.

I've been sitting in the sun and reading.

I read every day. My reading is done at night, in front of the tv where my hubby rules the remote, and other than a few shows, I usually read through the evening, finally snatching up the remote when he calls surrender and goes to bed.

But reading in a lounge chair in the sun? I've only done that on vacation at the beach. This past week, on nice days, I decided to grab the moment and do...nothing. Just read. Not worry that I haven't checked my email or trying to brainstorm this smaller project due soon. I've been letting my Muse rest and go unconscious until I can tempt her back out for a peek.

I go horseback riding. I really love it. Just me and the horse and learning things I always dreamed of.

I go out.

Let me repeat that please.

I go out. I met a girlfriend for lunch in Cold Spring. I do errands with no stress. I've had my eye doctor and dentist appointment.

My Muse is tired. I'm tired. I'm not working in an office filing or picking up the phone or filling out numbers on a spreadsheet. I'm forcing imaginary people to come alive on the page and sometimes, I have to give myself a break.

Write Free

My creative soul is not a factory worker. Deadlines are good, writing books is good, money is good, being in front of readers is good, but guess what?

Stopping is good, too.

To refill the well.

I'm beginning to realize doing nothing is also part of being a writer, because so much energy hums under the surface. We just don't see it. We can't point to our Muse and say: Look, she's working! I'm working! I promise I'm not being lazy!

Ridiculous, right? If we demanded more free time and termed it work in our heads, we wouldn't be uncomfortable trying to explain to people we're not just napping and people of leisure. That this is our job. And we shouldn't have to apologize for it.

Screw that. The cliché of refilling the well was created because if we suck out all the water and never dump any back in, there is only a hollow, echoey, dry space where nothing is nourished.

Let's make a promise to do more nourishing. Because when we're finally re-filled and ready?

Our stories will even more clear, fresh; and dazzling.

Chapter Eight

Typing The End and What Writers Do Next

I TYPED the end on my twenty-eighth book yesterday.

It's a short novella coming out for the Christmas holiday. This was a tough writing year. I wrote two big books back-to-back, finished a novella to wrap up the Searching for series, and then figured out I had to write this holiday story in two weeks. As usual, I overshot, thinking I could get more done than I should because I believe I have special super powers no one else has.

Umm, yeah. I don't. In fact, I'm as far from a superhero as Lex Luthor. I like to fiddle a lot, and watch too much Bravo television, and like naps, especially when I get stressed. Of course, I show up to my office every day, which is my job, but sometimes the writing doesn't go the way I imagined it should. Sometimes, I just puke words out in massive quantities in a panic, and found myself trapped in my pajamas for three days straight and no idea what's happening around me when I finally emerge from the cave.

I live a weird life.

Anyway, as I typed The End and cried – because somehow, some way, this story actually came out really good. I thought about how nice it was going to be to take a break. I gave myself one in July which lasted 2-3 weeks. It was heaven, but I figured with all that free time off, I'd return to my office dying to write. I figured my Muse would be itching to get back to work and produce a story of mastery because I'd given her so much free time to refill the well.

It kind of backfired.

I remember when my oldest son went to school for the first time. I was devastated. I collapsed in the driveway, sobbing, as he pulled away on the school bus.

I guess I was being a tad overdramatic because the

driver stopped and asked if I needed an ambulance.

When I returned to the house, I was broken hearted. I missed him. I wandered the empty rooms, picking up his stuffed animals, crying like he'd left for college, and eventually found my way back to my office. I still had my little one at home, and when I put him down for a nap, I figured I'd do a bit of work.

Hours later, I was pissed I had to go pick my oldest son up. Taking care of one child was so much easier than two! Add in pre-k and I had all this extra time I never imagined. Even better? They were both going back tomorrow! Hell, what had I been upset for? This was the best damn invention in the world of motherhood – SCHOOL!

I experienced the same type of issue after giving my Muse time off. She had gone on vacation and when I knocked politely, telling her we needed to write this Christmas story now, she raised her martini and said something really rude. She wasn't ready to go back. She'd gotten a taste of the good life, and damned if she was getting locked back up in the writing jail cell.

Let's just say she never really came back voluntarily. Like the bitch of a boss I am, I finally tossed out her cocktail and shoved her ass in the chair. Then we wrote the damn thing.

Today, we looked at the calendar, planning another mini vacation of cocktails and fun and discovered…

My next book is due on Halloween. And I have to start it ASAP. I have the weekend off, which will be filled with blog writing, and email catch up, and some promo, and copyedits. I scheduled an in-depth writing retreat with one of my besties next week so I could knock out some serious word count.

But here I am, back in the fire of deadlines. And here I am, promising myself next year will be different. I'll give myself more breathing room and space and be more relaxed with my writing schedule.

My Muse knows I'm a big fat liar. She's gone away and is in serious sulk mode. It's gonna get ugly next week when I tell her I plan to write 5K per day and won't accept anything less, especially since I'm removing all of my usual distractions.

Have I used my sacred blog space to whine about my life to you, my dear readers?

No. I just want to make a simple point.

It's not supposed to be easy. No one promised us easy. It doesn't matter what passion or job you are pursuing, from college to day jobs, our lives nowadays are spinning out of control with more and more responsibilities tacked on. We need to do more with less. We have little down time, and when we finally relax, most of us feel guilty.

When I imagined writing full-time, there was never any idea of what my challenges would be. In my mind, if I quit my job and got to finally write all day, it was a world of carousels, candy, and unicorns.

Everything looks better from a distance. We like to dream big but when we face unseen challenges, too many of us gripe or push back or even worse?

Quit.

The more I unearthed from this full-time job, the more realistic things got. Writing is my job. This is different from showing up on impulse and crafting magic when I want. I gave that up when I agreed to do this to pay bills.

I'm good with my part of the bargain. It's still better than a string of day jobs that sucked my soul and gave little back.

That being said, I know many writers who are successful and still have a job outside of writing. There is no one way to approach this career.

There is no one way of success. There is only the way that works best for you FOR NOW.

My only advice is for all of us to grab the moments. It's what's happening now—and when a good moment comes, just steep yourself in it. Be happy. When you take a break, push away the guilt, because I've also learned when the truck hits you, I doubt I'll regret I didn't write one more book.

I'd regret I didn't enjoy myself more, or spend time with my boys, or grab five minutes to watch the sunset. You don't need endless hours to find breathing space—all you need is a moment when you are completely present.

I'm going out to dinner tonight to celebrate finishing my book. I'm going to the movies with my boys this weekend.

And then I'll be back to work on Tuesday, doing a job I love more than anything.

Chapter Nine

"Your Baby is Ugly!" Let's Talk about Horrible Reader Reviews

EVER SINCE I penned my book, *Write Naked*, I've felt…naked. I've shared elements of my life as a writer I'd normally shy away from, but it was important I do what I advised because it made the difference between a good book and a bad book.

I think it was a good book. Others won't.

Which leads me to my big subject today.

Bad reviews.

You've heard writers compare their books to their babies, terrorized their precious child will be picked on, bullied, laughed at, and mocked. You've heard me also advise that when you are writing your book, it is truly your child. This child has not gone to school yet, or left the house. They've only been dropped at your sibling's or mother's house for a few precious hours so if there is advice to share, it's lovingly given.

Perhaps, it's a thoughtful tidbit to socialize your baby more; or give them a haircut, or other general instructions that are not threatening.

When your book is released to the world, you have no more control. You have to stand tall while your child is reviewed, analyzed, and ranked a certain number of stars. Maybe your child will be loved. Or slapped across the face. Or completely ignored.

Writers are known to struggle with bad reviews especially early on in their career. This makes sense, because the foundation is not as strong at this point. The writer doesn't yet realize if her books will make up an entire career, or if she can charm enough readers and reviewers to like her enough to read her next book. I am always extra gentle with new writers because they do need encouragement in a brutal world. Think of a parent who is kind but has a firm hand. You have to tell the truth, but there are many different ways to do it.

Write Free

Like in reviews.

I have written over thirty books. I have hit all the bestseller lists. I have been nominated as a RITA finalist. I have received beautiful reviews from authors I revere and still am humbled that they actually read something I've written. I've written a nonfiction book about writing. I've taught workshops and spoken at conferences.

But I still get bad reviews—some worse than others—and some when I'm not even looking.

Let me tell you what happened today.

I was going through my email when I stumbled upon a Google alert. It was linked to my name, and I saw that my book, Searching for Disaster, had been reviewed at a pretty big reader blog. This site was well-known and well respected. Everyone I knew read it or knew about it.

I remember pausing briefly, wondering if I was strong enough to read a cold review. I told myself it couldn't be bad. The book was amazing.

I clicked on the link.

Oh boy, it was bad.

I mean B-A-D. I was called out on using the "magical peen" and the "magical hoo ha" in romance. This is where the heroine cannot get the hero's magical penis out of her brain and vice versa which translates to a cheap maneuver to create emotional connection. They hated the way other characters were introduced from the series and how I sickeningly remind the reader that all my couples live in a happy ever after kingdom. The reviewer didn't like the way my hero talked about the puppies, or one of my favorite lines in the book that made my hero a chauvinistic, abusive asshole. The reviewer then said she was relieved it was over and that basically her time was wasted. Then there were a bunch of comments cheering her on, praising her review, and trashing my book, saying thank God they didn't have to read it.

Ouch.

Not gonna lie. I read that while my heart shredded in my chest, wondering how my book had gone so horribly, terribly wrong.

How did this happen?

I'd received stellar reviews and email regarding the emotional quality in that book. I poured a lot of myself in the struggle with drug addiction. I'd taken risks introducing a character who was extremely messy in the first chapter so readers can watch her grow and change.

I never believed I set up my hero to be abusive, or my heroine lived half of a life because she was always seeking a "magical peen."

I thought readers loved the puppies! My book was edited by a master in her field, who told me the book was one of her favorites.

But this reviewer HATED it and told in very clear detail how, and why she hated it.

I read the review over and over again. It was like poking a sore tooth.

I felt really bad for a while. I'm human. I questioned myself and my talent and the power of my story I'd believed in. I lost some time spinning out and wondering how I could've done better and made her like me. And like my books.

And then?

I let it go.

Earlier in my career, I couldn't have let it go. I would spend evenings crying over a review like this. There are reviews that say they don't like the book and why, and then there are reviews that gleefully tell in vivid detail how much they hated your book, and invite people to jump on board to share and celebrate the hate.

It feels awful. But in the bigger picture, a review is a review, and readers have a right to their opinions. And free speech. In any way they want to express it.

That's the beauty of the book world. There's good and there's bad. There are people who will never read your book and tell others to stay away. And there are people who will recommend your book like a loving friend to make someone happy. Many of the issues this reviewer had with my book is valid because that is her personal opinion. Writers cannot argue with opinion. It is the beauty of what we do. To put out any type of art, you will encounter many, many opinions.

An artist is not there to explain intentions. I couldn't read over her shoulder and point out my thoughts on why I wrote that scene or try to defend my choices. This reviewer hated my book for a dozen reasons and pointed each and every one out.

Fair enough.

Write Free

Is this post a subtle way to get revenge on a reviewer who tore me apart and make people feel bad for me?

No.

This is a post to let authors know this happens to everyone.

Some will hurt more than others. You must remember that eventually, you must go back to your writing.

You can still feel terrible. I hold a place deep inside where all my bitter and painful feelings from my bad reviews are boxed and locked up. I keep them away from my mind and my heart because it will destroy my ability to do my job.

My job is to write the best damn book I can. Not judge what will happen once the book is out in the world or how many people will hate it.

Do not let someone else's opinion affect how you feel about your work. Now, I must admit there are some reviews that have helped me a lot. They've pointed out weak spots in the book that I never saw, and I try to bring that constructive part into my new work, so I don't make the same type of mistakes. Nothing wrong with learning.

But other reviews will just be a difference in opinion. Where one reader swooned, another one got pissed off. To one reader, a hero is alpha and sexy. To another, he is abusive.

An author once told me she received a one star review citing the book was full of dirty sex.

The second review gave five stars and cited it was the best book ever because it was full of delicious, dirty sex.

One-star reviews can be good because it allows readers to narrow down what they do and don't like. One-star reviews can help us find our ideal readers faster.

That's cool.

If you are feeling a bit low, or particularly vulnerable, don't go read reviews. Don't click on the link. Don't go into the review muck of Goodreads (though I do like the site for many reasons and think the reviews are important there).

Just take a deep breath and go back to the writing.

Some days, we just feel stronger. You may want to see what's being said, and remind yourself to take it all in stride.

Write Free

Five-star reviews are forgotten.

One-star reviews are forgotten.

If you do your job, your story will not be forgotten. You will make many readers happy and that is the magic that drives us forward; to get naked and put ourselves out there.

For good. Or for bad.

Chapter Ten

How to Practice Writing Naked

It's odd how some days emotion lurks dangerously close to the surface, seeping through the skin and threatening to release in a flood of tears. The philosophies and circle of life is such a mix of joy and pain – that is why I write. There is no other way to sift through the mess and try to make some sense of it.

My mother-in-law lay in a hospital bed at seventy-eight years old. She had no health issues and went to the hospital for a broken rib.

She never got out.

The X-rays revealed kidney issues, which led to dialysis. This led to a stroke and a brain bleed and a stint in her brain. This led to feeding issues, and then pneumonia. Now she's in ICU and we don't know how long she has. My husband waits every day by his phone, dreading a call, the nights spent hoping sleep isn't broken by a professional, clipped voice telling him the news of her passing.

My son attended his first day of middle school. School is a reminder to me my children are on loan – though in my heart and bones they are all mine and I love them with a fierceness that would intimidate a mama bear. As my son got out of the car and walked toward the school, I realized I was on the timer. He is becoming his own person, learning the rules of society and figuring out who he is. What actions he can live with and which ones he can't. He'll make many mistakes and get his heart broken and I'll stand on the sidelines watching.

I've been crying most of the day allowing myself to feel the reality of my children growing up while my mother-in-law battles for life. Crying is damn freeing. It's my truth for this day, in this moment.

I think of my mother-in-law sending my husband off to school for the very first time. The clothes may have changed, the social environment and the schools are different, but the actions of letting go are timeless. Did her heart squeeze with pride and joy and sadness when he disappeared through that school door? Did she think of him grown up, with a family of his own, sending off his own children like I do right now? Did she memorize his crooked smile and big boy clothes and shiny new backpack and hold the image tight to her heart, positive she'd never forget it?

Today, I watched my dog sleep undisturbed when I entered the house. She never picked up her head because she didn't hear me. She's fourteen years old and half deaf. Her face is white and she has to go the bathroom more and she walks like her hips and joints ache. I think about when I got her as a puppy at eight weeks old, and how when I held her for the first time, she threw up all over me and I knew she was meant to be mine. I think of how she ate my furniture and curtains and most of my shoes and how she'd run so fast, no one could ever catch her. I think of how she lays on her leopard memory foam bed beside my desk every day while I write. And I wonder if I'll ever be able to write again if she leaves me.

I've been treasuring time with her lately, giving her extra bones and kisses and quality play, because when I see that beautiful white face look into mine with pure adoration, my heart feels like it'll break it's so full. I try not to think past the moment because it hurts too much.

Some things begin. Some things end. Some things continue.

Everything changes.

Take all of it – especially on those days when the mess is bubbling up like a pot of stew, spewing bursts of food against the walls, leaking over the stove, a bit out of control.

Take it and use it in the writing. This is the stuff that is human and real and true.

This is the stuff that must be on the page because it will translate to a great book.

Tomorrow I may wake up and feel none of this. I may look back and laugh at myself for feeling so vulnerable and emotional and silly.

But I don't want to forget. This day happened and it was real and it should be turned into something beautiful.

It should be turned into story.

Chapter Eleven

The Top Five Ways to Guarantee a Perfect Release Day

Ah, release days. Your book birthday. The day you send your baby into the world to be cooed over… or slaughtered. The day you realize it's time to let go—that your book no longer belongs to you and never will again.

I've had good release days and bad.

Want to know how to guarantee a good one?

Here's the secret sauce I've learned over the years!

- **Try not to obsess about ranking**

All writers out there are throwing slimy bananas or hard apples at me—trying to get me to take it back. Yes, it's almost impossible not to obsess about ranks on the day your book goes live, but it doesn't have to overtake every moment. I learn to check once in the morning, once in the afternoon, and once at night. No more—no less.

Because refreshing every single hour doesn't help your ranks or your mental health. By restricting it to the time you eat a meal, you limit the crazy. Or at least, you try.

Disclaimer: If you're tracking your ads, you will need to check numbers a bit more but you should have a limit. Don't pull an all-nighter, my loves.

- **Treasure the good reviews**

Do you know how many times I'll skim over a good review, pat myself on the back, and then go obsess for hours over the bad? Dude—that's just not good. As humans, we've learned to relish the crappy and throw away the good, and release day is the time to reverse all that bad karma. Now, I gather every good review in a file with the link and some noteworthy quotes. Not only is it fabulous to go to when I feel like I'm tanking this writing career – but it reminds you how hard you worked, and how your story is touching people out there.

Strangers. People who love your book and think you are worthy. When did this get so hard for us to accept?

- **Celebrate**

Some release days, I'd wave off my hubby and say I needed to stay hunched over my computer. I convinced myself I needed to endlessly check social media accounts, comment on every post, and not leave my office.

Then one day, I woke up. Hell—if I'm not going to celebrate my book birthday – who else will? It's a time to take one lousy day out of our lives and tell ourselves we are valuable. We don't get that feedback as often as day jobs. We need to claim it for ourselves. Go to dinner, threaten your husband to send you flowers, eat chocolate, drink champagne. Feel fabulous. People all over the world dream of becoming a "real" writer – and we are. How wonderful is that?

- **Be grateful**

Instead of belly aching about your rank or how author A had an easier shot at reaching top 100 because of this, that, or the other thing – just take a breath and thank your lucky stars you published a book. Thank the people who email you or comment. Take an hour of release week and answer your fans, share other author's accomplishments, be part of this community we mostly love and adore. Gratitude changes our mental state and reminds us of the good we have in our lives. It brings a rush of powerful energy. We need to be grateful for the writing.

- **Promote other authors**

Release day is like a sisterhood. Instead of greedily grabbing the spotlight, take some time to help shout out other releases from other authors. Read another author's book and give them a review or a blurb. Remind yourself no one can do it alone – success is so much better with people cheering you on along the way. If you're feeling jealous, or down because another author is doing so much better in the ranks than you are, turn it around by giving them a shout out. Buy the book. Do a share. Comment on a post that's tagged them. You'll be amazed at how much better you feel by draining the jealousy poison and truly opening yourself up to helping others.

Try to remember whatever you have right now is meant for you.

Whatever you don't have is something you don't need. But it doesn't mean it's not in your future! Watching other authors accomplish big things is a reminder the same stuff can happen to you. It's opening up more opportunities in our industry.

Step into your book release day with passion, gratitude, and celebration.

God knows, writing the book was hard work!

Chapter Twelve

The Top Facts About Author Signings

I'm off to Denver for the first Book Bonanza signing and thinking about the author signings. They are getting more and more popular for authors, and sprouting up in so many states, authors now have a huge selection to pick from.

I try to do my best to hit different geographical locations each year so I can meet the most readers possible. This past year, I've already done Rome, this week is Denver, and in September I'll be in NYC and Kentucky.

Signings can get expensive, though, so authors need to be careful about which ones they decide on, and why. Most of the time, financially, I come out in the hole. Even with no table fees, and the books I sell, the amount for plane fare, taxis, eating, and miscellaneous (like the famous bar bill lol!) is way over what I make in book royalties. Also, my time away from my office is expensive. I could be using those days to write a new book, which is the fastest and most economical way to make more money in a writing career. I'm old now, too, so when I return, I usually need a minimum of 2-3 days of downtime, shoveling out from my administrative duties before I can even think about getting back to writing.

So, what do I really get back from attending an author signing?

Let's go over them.

Networking:

Most signings will have other authors attending that will make you fan girl. One of the best parts is scrambling around to each table, getting to meet so many authors face-to-face and get your own signed books and swag. There are usually dinners or reader parties so you get to network, meet new people, and get a fresh vision of the writing world.

I always come home with a bunch of new friends I adore, my social media followers explodes, and I'm introduced to new work from authors I haven't read before. One on one conversations have been game changers for me. I've learned important information, made new contacts, and received opportunities I never would've been offered.

Everyone is always super friendly and welcome. It's scary when you don't know many other authors. I remember not wanting to leave my room and having panic attacks, overcome by social anxiety. But every time I took a deep breath and forced myself to go out there, I came back giddy with excitement and buzzing with possibility, bonding with new friends. I promise you won't regret it.

Travel Opportunities:

I love to use author signings to see places I've never been before. It's a tax write-off, you can take your assistant or a friend/spouse/child, and tack on a few days in the front or back of the signing for vacation. I've been to places I would have never chosen and am really grateful. Make sure you leave the hotel! I've made the mistake of becoming so involved with the events, I only glimpsed the airport and local restaurants. Book some type of tour or sightseeing event. Experience the local cuisine. Grab a few authors you've never hung out with and tag along. Don't be afraid to ask—when I was brave and questioned what another group was doing, they invited me to join them. I've met the coolest people that way!

Meeting Readers:

Simply put, meeting my readers is a priceless experience. I write in isolation, for a nameless, faceless public. But when I get to see a reader up close, my mind is blown. When I'm thanked for my stories, or experience excited squeals, or shy requests to take a picture, I'm reminded of what I do this for. I've had readers apologize for carting around a box of dog eared, well-loved backlist books for me to sign. And I tell them it's the coolest thing in the entire world.

I get all mushy and happy inside. Suddenly, all those hours of struggling with my character and my stories are worth it. Suddenly, I'm not worried about my sales, or if my latest book is tanking, or if I'll be able to wrestle my current story into submission. I'm just humbled that a real live person is freaking out over a book I wrote. It gives me a reset in my mind. It motivates me to keep going and do better, because I just met a person who is reading my stuff. I'm reminded my stories are important.

There is nothing more inspirational than talking to readers.

This past month when I travelled to Rome for RARE, my husband was my assistant. Afterward, slumped in the chair, hand numb, exhausted beyond measure for signing for more than eight straight hours, he looked at me with a new expression on his face I've never seen before.

"I think I took 300 pictures of you," he said in awe, shaking his head. "I saw a reader cry. And you got gifts! Good gifts! They love you."

He got to see the Coliseum and the Vatican and eat pasta and pizza and stroll the ancient streets. But when I asked him what his favorite part was, he told me the signing, because he'd never experienced something that amazing. He was proud of me.

Pretty damn cool, huh?

A few tips for authors?

You will be completely drained by the end of the day. After these big signings, I feel as if I need to sleep for days. Listen to your body and do what you can. I do find if I push through and share a meal with other authors after the signing, I'm recharged and grab valuable networking time.

But since each one of us is unique in how "peoply" we can be, and our energy drains in different ways, don't apologize for taking care of yourself. Better to expect and prepare with extra hydration, going to sleep at a decent hour, and grabbing some alone time in your room between events. Usually, the last night I order room service and stay in bed eating fries.

Many authors don't know what to bring. Tables will usually be there and set up but everything else is on you. You should order a tablecloth with your author brand, or a standing banner. There will be a bunch of authors and you need to stand out.

Bring swag, preferably with your author or book branding. I can do a whole post on my history with swag, but I usually focus on my current release and have an item that blends with it. For instance, in my Italy series, I ordered stickers that say Meet me in Italy, along with matching pop sockets. When I was writing my Searching for series, I owned a bright yellow tablecloth with the moot: What are YOU searching for in your romance? Then I had a bunch of book covers listed underneath.

I've done pens, mini book magnets, tote bags, t-shirts, keychains, stickers, postcards, and bookmarks. Candy on the table is a great draw to get readers to stop and chat. Pairing swag with what fits the book series stands out.

Now, a few tips for the readers who come to this.

Yes, we are tired, and have signed endless books, but when you get to my table, I'm meeting you for the first time. I'm excited. I'm humbled. I'm grateful you read my books. I love fangirling and love talking about my books. Tell me your favorite couple, or book, or series. Ask me questions. Give me a hug (I'm Italian we hug everyone). Take a pic. Tag me on Facebook. Tag me everywhere.

This is why I'm here. For you. When you drag in that carton of books and apologize profusely, I'm in sheer heaven. I love signing your books. I love interacting with you. I wish I had more time, but I will make sure I use those precious few minutes the best way possible, so you feel special.

Because, my readers, all of you are.

After all, you made my dream come true.

Sign on, peeps.

Chapter Thirteen

A Writer's Truth

I WAS DRIVING HOME from dinner with my boys and peeked in the rear-view mirror.

My youngest had rested his head in my older son's lap. My older son was looking down at him with a tender expression, stroking his hair. The evidence of brotherly love was carved into my son's features, and I felt my heart explode in my chest and splinter into too many pieces. At that moment, I realized I was looking at the symbol of everything good in my life. My two boys, loving each other, at peace. Safe.

I knew it was a moment to treasure because it would change in a heartbeat. It was full of fragility.

But damned if I didn't hold that moment as tight as a Mama bear could, and hug it into my very memory.

That, my peeps, is a mother's truth.

I've read amazing books from authors who have been able to express that type of emotion and what those fleeting moments mean. How being a parent allows you to be the very best of yourself…and the worst. How to love another human being so much it's an actual physical pain and fear that never goes away. Motherhood is full of so many complicated emotions, I could write about it the rest of my life and never tire or get bored.

My newest release, *The Charm of You*, hits all retailers this week. It was a beautiful book to write because it was a gift. I've been struggling with writing lately so this story not only flowed, but reminded me of how joyous my work can be.

Yesterday, I received a message from one of my readers who scored an advanced copy. Besides gushing about how much she loved the book, she took the time to highlight a particular passage that struck her. She used the hashtag #truth. I could tell it had affected her and she'd remember that line.

This is what it said:

"I think we forget to stop and experience the totality of what we're given, you know? I don't want to waste my time. I want to pause and revel in the physical and emotional pieces of my moments, even if they're jagged and sometimes painful." She paused as if picking through her thoughts to better describe herself. He held his breath, studying the flickering expressions on her beautiful face. "Books make it easy to feel and be vulnerable. That's probably why I love reading so much."

When I re-read those words I'd written, I was struck by the truth. Yes, I'd written it from the viewpoint of my heroine, but it's something I believed in my soul. The passage had come out in my work, to share with the world, without my knowledge. I was able to funnel such deep feelings and emotions because I always try to write with my heart and soul open.

I write naked.

I count myself humbled to be in the small percentage of the world that is able to share words and stories that may be relevant to others. Artists, teachers, lecturers can all share such a gift. We must treasure this ability. Hone it. Sharpen it. Practice it. Embrace it.

These are the moments that make a difference. The moments we tuck into ourselves to take out and mull over; treasure; re-live in the dark days or endless nights when we feel alone and need something to cling to.

It's our truth.

Be proud to share your truth with the world.

After all, this is a writer's job. Treat it with care because these things may be strong, but they are also incredibly fragile and fleeting.

Doesn't this make it worth treasuring?

Doesn't this make it worth sharing?

I say, hell yes.

Go write your truth. Not tomorrow, or next week. Right now.

We need it.

Chapter Fourteen

The Most Powerful Word in the English Language

I REMEMBER HANGING with my family one afternoon, and we were going around the table asking about our favorite and least favorite words. Of course, every time my family gets together there's a lot of food, wine, laughs, and smart-talk. We also play a mean game of scrabble. I remember one of my best friend's mentioning to me I'd never find Mr. Right unless it was a pizza delivery guy, because every Friday night I'd go to my parents' house to play Scrabble!

So, my brother pipes up and says his favorite word is hope.

It took me aback. My brother isn't the touchy feely type, and rarely displays much emotion. When I questioned him further, he said that he's seen miracles in life happen, and some of the truly best actions from human beings all revolve around hope.

I loved his response. I don't think I told him though. I probably grunted and moved on, but his words always stuck with me, because I believe the same thing.

That's why I write romance novels.

I was born to write romance. I was lucky to know at twelve years old romance writing was my True North and destiny. I smiled and shook my head thousands of times when confronted by many, many people on the question, "When are you going to write a real book?"

I'd always answer: "I have. A dozen of them. Go buy one!"

Romance is the realest type of book you can read, because it focuses on the human condition of my favorite word: love. And the guaranteed happy ending gives readers something that is beyond priceless in this very brutal, painful world we live in.

Hope.

Why shouldn't we believe in love? In the power of goodness over evil? In the kindness of strangers? In the beautiful chemistry and passion of lovemaking?

Romance novels reflect everything I want to live my life around, and I never apologize for it. I brag about it, along with my husband who will tell anyone and everyone he meets that his wife writes romance, and he will ask strangers if they like romance novels without even a blush.

Yeah. That's why I married him.

I've always been intrigued by the ruckus romance novels inspire, especially about an ending that leaves a reader uplifted instead of train wrecked by a death or tragedy. But reading romances has taught me something else that no one really thinks of. We are so focused on the endings, but romance novels are really about happy beginnings.

Remember that feeling when you are attracted to someone and butterflies jump in your stomach? Remember the first time you realized you were falling in love, and were overcome by excitement and terror in equal amounts? Remember that first kiss that you replayed in your mind over and over like a delicious secret you couldn't get enough of? Remember that first vow, or your first fight, or your first baby?

It's really about firsts. The ending is just a way for a reader to breathe a sigh of pure satisfaction and happiness. The reader already knows there's so much in store for the couple. Domestic bliss and hell, pain, tragedy, joy, family, turning points, grief. It's all wrapped up in a romance because two people in love become a couple who struggle through this world together.

And that, my lovelies, needs a heck of a lot of hope.

My brother is a doctor now, and he deals with hope every day in the medical field. I deal with hope on the page. We all need more of it to make this world a more beautiful place.

I write romance, and I shout it to the rooftops. I never hide my paperbacks, and I never fluster when someone asks if I write those Fabio love stories.

I have a master's in English Literature, been at the top of my game in the business world, and lecture workshops on writing in all venues. I think romance authors and readers are the most brilliant, brave, hopeful people in the world.

Let's all hope together for more love in the world in all formats.

Chapter Fifteen

All About Character

My son wore Spiderman pajamas to school. They had wings. They were way too small on him and hit about mid-calf. They were similar to footie pajamas since they were one piece, but without the actual feet.

He's in middle school. Not elementary.

Yeah.

See, when he informed me of his plan to wear them for pride week, I kind of panicked. I was terrified of him being made fun of. I asked if anyone else at school was going to wear those types of pajamas. I tried to explain they were too small for him so he'd change his mind.

My son just shrugged the whole thing off. Said he thought it was pretty cool, and he was wearing them. He didn't care what anyone else did.

I spoke to his brother and asked him if he thought it was a good idea. My second son shot me a look, and said, "If he's comfortable, why aren't you?"

Good question. Because from my experience in middle school, if I did something as brave and cool and unique as that, I'd end up being bullied and humiliated and forced to move out of state. But guess what? That's my experience. I was a shy, awkward, terrified kid who had her nose stuck in a book and jerked when a stranger said hello to me. I was a mess.

My son went to school in his Spiderman pajamas. When he got on the bus no other child was wearing pajamas. I felt sick to my stomach all day, worried about him.

When he came home, he was happy. Said he played basketball with a huge group of boys and when he swished it in, they told him he had Spidey powers. He got high fives. Other kids wore unicorn and Hello Kitty footies to school and they all shouted in the hallway when they passed each other.

I almost cried. From relief, and pride, that somehow my son had the strength of character to just be who he is. He's told me he's gotten hurtful comments before on some of his choices, but he doesn't care. He tells me those people are not his friends, so what does it matter?

OMG. Yes. He's teaching me more lessons than a therapist.

Now, let's switch to writing, which is the whole point of this lovely post.

I believe character is one of the most important things you can do to make your story explode off the page. I write about this extensively in my book, *Write Naked*, but since I've got 4K to write today and the words are coming slow, I figured I'd distract myself by a short post about it.

It's very important to know who your character is. The beauty of this is that every person is different, and so is your hero and heroine. One book, you may be writing about a powerful, assertive, savvy business woman with a quick temper and a drive to success. Another book may feature a an awkward, shy bookworm who's battling to learn social skills and kiss a boy. Their pasts are different. So are their viewpoints, likes, dislikes, and goals.

Write Free

This is the key for your story. The plot can be anything if you sketch out fascinating, dynamic, interesting, flawed characters who resonate with readers.

If you're having trouble getting them sketched out on the page, use my son as an example. Use your mother, your friends, your husband, and your children. Pull on those experiences where you've met people who make you wonder what makes them tick. Tug the loose thread, make it unravel, and get messy.

I would sketch out my son as a hero who doesn't fit into the usual job category – he thinks outside the box. He's fearless because he's comfortable with who he is. He pushes boundaries. He's loyal to a fault, because if he keeps his word, he assumes someone else will, which leads him eventually to disappointment in others. He's been in love with a girl since second grade and dreamed of taking her to the prom when he hit high school. Senior year, he realizes his dream and picks her up in a stretch limo, and gives her a single red rose instead of the usual corsage, and they dance slow, rather awkwardly in the high school gym with balloons and streamers hanging from the ceiling and he realizes he loves her.

He follows her to college and they have a passionate love affair but after graduation, she wants to move to Hollywood to be an actress and he wants to stay in New York where there's actual seasons and snow for Christmas and not swarming with fake tans and fake people. They begin fighting, tearing each other apart, and finally break up to go separate ways. He falls into a deep depression and vows to never give his entire heart and soul to another woman again. He settles in New York and years later, gets engaged to a very nice, very sweet woman he thinks he loves. Later on, he comes face to face with his first love. They are both engaged to others. But the moment he sees her again, he knows he must do everything to get her back, because he will have only half a life without her, so he makes a grand gesture and asks her to choose him, and she does, but they leave a big mess behind, people who are heartbroken and betrayed and have to pick up their own shattered lives. They get married, try to have children, are challenged by fertility, and their relationship begins to erode. They separate years later, come back together, and adopt a child. They travel on great adventures together, raise their daughter, and then one day, are faced with the ultimate choice that affect the rest of their lives. What is it, you ask? Well, it's---

Hell, I don't know, this was just a rough example.

Is this my son's story? Nope. He's only 13. I have no idea what's going to happen, but if you start with a foundation, or a big choice, or the point where everything they thought they wanted in life is completely lost, you can begin to figure them out, and then you can follow the story.

My characters are never fully known to me until the last portion of the book. Like clockwork, I receive the AHA! Moment, and then I go back to layer and fix all the scenes where I struggled because I didn't know who he or she was yet. For me, writing the book is a journey to creating a full character.

But God knows, you have to start with something. Use the world around you for the push off.

Now, let me get back to my book.

Remember, my peeps. Don't just write.

Write Naked.

Peace out.

Chapter Sixteen

A Writer's Perspective on Story

A Star is Born is the best movie of the year.

In my opinion, of course.

Besides the acting and the music, there were themes that resonated with me as a creative artist. The most moving was the speech Sam Elliot gave to Lady GaGa when he was speaking about music. Here it is:

"Music is essentially 12 notes between any octave. 12 notes and the octave repeats. It's the same story, told over and over. Forever. Only thing the artist can offer the world is how they see those 12 notes.
"

Mind blown.

Write Free

In the romance genre, we are consistently told to think outside the box and bring a "fresh" take to a trope. Yet, there is not anyone who can claim a completely original story. We all use the same tropes to spin our view of the story, from friends-to-lovers, enemies-to-lovers, makeovers, billionaires, best friend's little sister, best friends' older brother, revenge, etcetera.

Everything's been done. This should not disappoint you. This should free you from these crushing expectations marketing, editors, and publishers try to place on your shoulders. Sometimes, there's an easy hook to spin to help grab readers' attention. Sometimes, it's not as clear-cut to pick out one particular piece of the story to use as the hook to sell the sucker.

But I want to talk about story—not selling. And this quote from the movie reminds us all that the only thing you can bring to your book is your personal imprint. The way you see those same notes. Your individual perspective on the world and how you view it.

Transferring it from our minds to the page is the challenge. Like writing a song using the same twelve notes, there is a formula to story we shouldn't be afraid of. Use the framework and be unique with your imprint. There are a million options and paths a character can choose, and each decision leads to a new outcome.

Structure is good. The challenge?

Use the structure to frame your story, but break open the guts of it and be brave. Take risks. Push characters. Push yourself. How do you view love? Pain? Growth? Loss? How do you grieve? How is your character different from any of the other stories you've read?

Most of the time, I don't usually find these important nuggets out until at least halfway through my book. My process is a journey of discovery, and then after the crap is on the page in all its glorious mess, I go back and realize there are plenty of gold nuggets to pick out. That's when I layer. Add/delete/tweak scenes depending on what I've revealed about the characters. I make sure there's a growth arc, and that he/she has changed on the last page from the person we met on the first page.

Twelve notes.

One structure.

Endless possibilities based on your perspective.

Write Free

When you begin to doubt and think your story isn't special—that it's all been done before—look in the mirror.

You are special, therefore, so is your story. Sure, it may suck in first draft, or even third draft, but never doubt you have something important to say that the world needs to hear.

Use your notes.

We're waiting to hear them.

Chapter Seventeen

The Top 5 Reasons Why You Should Do Your Own #Nanowrimo

I'VE BEEN deep in the cave. I had to finish a book due, and this story ended up surprising me, so when I thought I was finished, my characters decided they weren't ready to leave, so I wrote 20K more.

I needed them to finally go away.

Each book that's due, I lie to myself. I outline the perfect schedule, writing an average of 2-3K per day, adding in a dash of family, a sprinkle of errands, and the occasional disaster. I always come out with a sparkling, clean proposal with plenty of days off and the delivery of the manuscript early.

Imagine that.

Unfortunately, I've had this fantasy for the last thirty books because I learned early, I'm a sick adrenaline junkie who likes to wait to the very last moment, and then go screaming and bitching into my office, pumping out 5-6K a day while I rant to everyone around me and ask HOW DID THIS HAPPEN TO ME AGAIN?

My son had the nerve to ask me if I had been wearing the same clothes for three days in a row.

I whispered the word, DEADLINE, and he slowly backed out of the room, and threw me a leftover piece of Halloween candy like a rabid dog.

But I wanted to talk about National Writing Novel Month (NANOWRIMO)– not my screwed-up writing life.

The premise is to write 50K in thirty days. I participated in this movement for many years, but NANOWRIMO is now officially closed due to some serious issues. The original organization is no longer active, but the concept remains widely practiced. I kept the original title of this essay because the term is still well-known.

But it's the practice I want to focus on here. Not the organization.

I'd encourage authors to try it. Just once.

Participating in this challenge when I was an unpublished author was key to helping me create a habit of being able to write on a daily basis. It taught me that no matter what happens around me, I made a commitment to my writing, and it was not going to come in second. Not in November.

Nanowrimo taught me to vomit words and deal with fixing that shit later. Words beget more words. Work begets more work. We have nothing to sell or make money on or market if we don't have words on the page, that makes stories.

Nanowrimo taught me to take myself seriously. Writing needs to be an investment of time and dedication and care. You need to stand up and declare you are a writer, and will be writing. For the month of November, you go into survival mode. Cleaning, cooking, socializing with friends, watching movies with the kids, all of it goes to the back burner for thirty days. Make a deal with your spouse or partner so they'll support you in November and you'll make it up to them in December.

It's time to claim your dreams. Goals are necessary to achieving dreams. Don't wait for anyone else to tell you that. It has to come from you or no one is going to listen.

Nanowrimo stripped away my writer's block. Basically, I had no more time for it. If I struggled for too long on a page, or a chapter, I learned to blast through or start a new scene. It helped me experiment and figure out what worked best for me if I got stuck. Before, I would've left the pages to linger for days, while I went to figure things out. When you need to write a book in a month, you have no such luxury. You need to figure it out now. I began to skip around and work on different scenes. My usual process is to be a linear writer, but to get words on the page, I tried new things. It helped blast the story forward.

It helped me form an important habit. Every day, I had to open the manuscript. I had to face the blank page. I had to create words.

Nanowrimo taught me to trust myself. All you have is you, your book, and a keyboard. There's no one else in the room, and you need to depend on yourself and your Muse to get you to the finish line. That is an act of pure trust and faith. When you see what you accomplished in those thirty days, you learn you can do things that are hard. And trust me, writing is hard. This is good practice.

Instead of worrying or planning or overthinking, just mark out a certain amount of time—7 days, 30 days—and begin writing. Who cares if you don't have a plot or an outline or a carefully written schedule? Show up every day, anyway.

What if your terrified Muse goes into hiding?

Trick her. Sit down and begin writing and she may peek her head out and screech, "What are you doing? I'm not ready for this yet!" But you will just quietly ignore her, keep working, and eventually she may help you because she has no choice.

Make your writing a priority. This is a great challenge to do if you feel as if you've been spending too much time on marketing or admin, and want to focus on words.

There have been a few organizations to step up and offer programs or challenges to take the place of NANOWRIMO. I've listed a few below to check out, though I haven't done any of them yet or know the founders.

One last tip? Create your own challenge! Bring in a few friends, target a month, set your goals, and commit.

Organizations & Challenges:

- AutoCrit Novel 90 Writing Challenge
- StoryADay
- Shut Up & Write
- Pathfinders Writing Collective
- 4thewords
- myWriteClub

There are many more so do your research and pick what feels right to you.

Chapter Eighteen

On Not Writing

I cannot believe another year has passed.

With Thanksgiving behind, and Christmas barreling up, it's hard not to compare this December to last year. It was right after I lost my father, and I had begun to spiral. I had two huge books due that I needed to start writing, and I'd become completely unable to write for the first time in my life.

After an intervention with my friend and publisher, Liz Berry, I realized I had to step away for a while and not even try. I was too raw and broken and needed to heal. My Muse was silent and she needed to rest and figure stuff out in order to make sense of my new day-to-day life. So, I took the month and spent hours watching tv, huddled under a blanket. I spent time with my kids and my dog. I didn't write.

One month turned into three. Grieving is on its own schedule, no matter how much I craved control. I had to juggle deadlines and push off projects but I have no regrets. I have learned we need to trust our bodies and minds if they scream for a time-out.

One year later, I just turned over my newest book to the editor, and have two weeks free before my second round of revisions come in. Between second and third rewrites, and copyedits, I'll be busy enough not to feel guilty.

But I have an entire 14 days left. Free.

Well, kind of.

When I crawl out of my office after delivering a book, it takes me a while to adjust. I'm like the mole who's been living in darkness in the hole, and when the creature crawls out, he's blind for a while. After I became human again, and learned how to speak and see people, I realized I had hours of admin work to catch up on. Emails never returned; blog posts to write; social media to update.

I dug in and though it's a daily beast, I caught up.

Now, let me set the scene.

I put the kids on the bus. Make my coffee. Carry it to the office. And….

Do nothing.

I made long lists of all the things I want to accomplish before my next round of edits. My task list looks something like this:

Create and test new FB ads

Post for full week at Author's Exchange FB group where I'm hosting

- Compose newsletter for 12/13
- Book travel for next signing
- Gather audio samples for Steele Brothers project
- Install new keyboard
- New post for Books and Main
- Complete front and back matter for new book
- Gather teasers for new book
- New AMS ads for German *Charm of You*
- Xmas cards. Do I want to do them this

year? My mother's bothering me—I may have to?
- Write new blog post *thank God I'm doing this now*

Glamorous, right?

Besides my task list, I have a dead few months in between with no releases so I planned to write either a new novella, or short from one of my previous series. I wanted to give my readers new content.

I have a huge announcement coming soon regarding my next project, and since I'll be writing a lot next year, it would be smart to get ahead and begin creating some character outlines, research, or something so when January 1st rolls around I won't be in panic mode.

Guess what I decided to do?

Nothing.

Yes, this is probably not good advice but I'm sticking to my plan and defending it to the critics who say you should always be moving hard toward your goals and your dreams; and an object in motion stays in motion; and all those wonderful pieces of advice that inspire you to get off your ass and just do it!

But I don't want to do anything. I want to nap, and read, and spend time with my kids. I want to do online shopping and lunch with a friend and finish some of my Netflix series.

Last December, I had no choice. I couldn't work. I was burnt.

This December, I choose not to work. Because I want to take a break and enjoy myself for absolutely no reason. Edits will be enough. Keeping up with social media will be enough. Responding to email will be enough.

This time, it feels good. I'm choosing not to feel guilty or lazy or like an amoeba. My workaholic tendencies are so ingrained, I struggle throughout my life between crazy bursts of madness and endless work, and then days of pure laziness because I'm too burnt out to function.

This month, I'm trying to balance.

Soon, it will be a new year. I need to ponder what my mantra word will be—my theme and vision for the upcoming year. I like to create lists and work on my planner and dive deep into goals and dreams I want to manifest.

My point to this long, blabbering, me-centric post?

If you want to take some time off, do it. Don't apologize, don't explain, and don't feel guilty. We forget we are not working in an office doing filing or data entry. We are creative artists. We really do need space to do nothing.

The best part? I feel like I'm not working but I really am. My Muse is sifting through ideas, stories, moments and figuring out where they will be placed in my future stories. She's playing. I'm living and resting and thinking. I'm becoming whole again so I can go back out and attack the great big world with a ferocious roar.

Today, I'm just going to not write.

Chapter Nineteen

The Alpha Male Problem in the #MeToo Movement

I LOVE alpha males in romance novels.

They make me swoon. They make me shiver. They make me close my eyes with the thrill of the scene. I love them in sweet romances, dark romances, and erotic romances. They can command a kiss, or still the heroine with a dominant stare. They can be possessive and seethe with touch-her-or-die vibes. It's one of my favorite things reading romance.

Yet, I do adore writing a good beta hero now and then. A nerdy, geek who transforms into his power. A sweet single Dad who makes my heart melt when he deals with his child. The gentle nature of a friends to lovers situation, allowing the heroine to slowly open up to the possibility of more.

In this current world where books are banned and every action is judged, alpha males have definitely been ripped apart. Romance fans are back to defending our right to read what we want without societal constrictions.

Are were really back to the days where women are blamed for not knowing reality from fiction? Are we still using Fabio and rape romances as the standard? When, for God's sakes, are we finally going to move on?

This is the #METOO climate. Before, readers were totally accepting of secret work romances; of bosses forcing secretaries to service them in all ways; where rules were not something anyone had to worry about when writing bossholes.

Now, many writers pause in distress and wonder if they need to outline to the reader that consent was applied. Or slip in a relaxed workplace rule to allow leeway. It's like the old argument with the condom during a sex scene—does your hero need to sheathe every time or can we just forget about it because it's fictional?

I go back and forth. The alpha males I write sometimes bow to the rules, sometimes ask for consent, and sometimes…not. I've balanced these changes from my prior work by being super clear to the readers what I'm writing.

Being clearer with triggers can be a way to get around these limitations. You can list trigger warnings now on publishing pages and in the beginning of your book. Being clear with cover, genre, and tone is important. Knowing your audience is key. Depending on what I release, I let my newsletter know if there's cute rescue dogs or a BDSM dungeon. You can also funnel email segments to blast our certain stories to certain audiences.

Remember the scene in the movie, Tootsie? Jessica Lange tells Dustin Hoffman what she really dreams about is a man to tell her in plain, brutal language that he basically finds her attractive and would love to sleep with her instead of leading her through an exhausting game she didn't want to deal with.

And remember when Dustin Hoffman approaches her at a party and utters every exact word she said she wanted to hear?

Write Free

Remember when she slapped him?

That's what I'm talking about. Fiction belongs in fiction for a reason. Women are intelligent and can tell the difference. When I read a murder mystery, I don't assume the nice guy is hiding a serial killer persona. And if you're working with a guy, I'm sure you don't expect him to suddenly throw you on the desk and hike up your skirt because he deems you a bad girl.

Except…YUM.

Rules are always changing with fiction, including restrictions or societal norms. We can still write badass alpha holes as long as we are clear what we are doing, and our audience knows what they are getting.

Fiction is an escape, and readers are all different in what types of heroes and stories they love to read to experience that ultimate escape.

Now, I have to go because my husband just made dinner and he's calling me.

That's my reality.

For now, I'll leave my alphas to the pages of my book!

Chapter Twenty

Going Home

RECENTLY, I went with my boys to see *A Dog's Way Home*. We were looking for a family movie to entertain us on a rainy Saturday afternoon, and though the preview looked a bit cheesy, we figured we'd give it a try.

Buckets of tears later, I admit I didn't see the emotion of this movie coming. The plot is simple enough: a dog named Bella (which happens to be the name of my dog!) tries to find her way home to her owners after being sent away temporarily while they get a new house in order. Of course, the dog doesn't know she's not being abandoned, so she decides to take control and find her way home. The movie goes on to detail the dog's many adventures in the miles she travels along with her various experiences with people and other animals.

What affected me so much about the movie was the emotion. I'm always urging writers to open up a vein and bleed on the page to inflict as much emotion as possible for the reader—without going into melodrama. The relationships Bella formed were real—from her adopted mother, to a baby mountain lion, to a group of ragtag dogs on the hunt for food. We are shown that some people are only meant to be in our lives for a little while. Others are meant to be with us forever.

There are lessons to learn from every encounter in life—some beautiful, and many so painful we feel as if we'll collapse underneath its weight. We meet some characters to lighten our load and make us laugh. And others are meant to be our soul-mates, whether in love or friendship. There are good people and bad. But the goal is to find that special place or person that completes us.

Yes, we need to be complete on our own first. But finding that special person we can be ourselves with, open up to, and be vulnerable in showing our love is a precious gift. Bella recognized her gift immediately, and searched hundreds of miles outside her comfort zone to find it again.

These big emotions made me think about the book I was writing, and my own life. Reminded me to try and be real and true and open. Sometimes, it becomes easy to bury myself in work and remain isolated from the outside world. I become my own world when I'm involved in a book and time blurs around me. It's important to remember we need to experience relationships with others so we can continue to grow and experience new things and bring our stories to the page. This keeps us fresh. It keeps us accountable to the trueness of the work.

I also believe we have many homes throughout our lives. Sometimes, they change—from your childhood home steeped with past memories, to the college dorm surrounded by other students, all the way to our first real apartment as we scrape for rent and proudly throw house parties with our friends; to our "grown-up" house where we may welcome a husband, children, and cook actual meals in a kitchen. They all blur together in my memory but each has a unique stamp—a right of passage in my life that defined what home meant to me.

I've been writing a series entitled STAY, and exploring the theme of home in each of the books.

I've loved watching each of my characters struggle with finding their right path, and the choices love allowed them to make. Some knew who they were and where they belonged from the beginning. Others didn't figure it out until the very end.

Using home as a key theme in your work can help you dig deeper into the story and motivations of your hero and heroine. Watching a simple dog movie ended up becoming a beautiful surprise—an opportunity for me to think about my journeys of home, and the ones my boys will embark on later in life, while I watch from the sidelines.

We may not have any magic red ruby slippers, but as the Good Witch said, we always had the power to go home, anyway.

All we have to do is create it.

Chapter Twenty-One

How To Write a Book

It's time to share the secret sauce writers have been protecting for years.

Yes, I'm finally going to spill the beans and let the world in on the actual steps you need to follow in order to write a book. We've kept our careers shrouded in secrecy, banking on your questions of "How do you get your ideas?" and "Why do writers look ugly and scared of people?" to distract you from figuring out how to become a real author.

But I'm tired of being selfish. It's time I open the vault so all of us can begin to write full-time, be successful, make buckets of money, and get a cool nameplate that screams AUTHOR.

Write Free

Ready? Here we go:

Butt in chair.

Open up a blank Word document (or any type of blank page you can type or write on)

Write crappy words for endless hours until something resembling a story eventually appears.

When your brain is fried and your fingers hurt, get up and walk around. Refill coffee. Talk to your dog. Channel surf through talk shows and reality tv in complete fascination. Spend the next half hour trying to force yourself to go back into your prison – aka- your office.

Go back and repeat step #3

Eat. Have some interaction with family members. Sleep.

Rinse and Repeat.

Buy my book, *Write Naked: A Bestseller's Secrets to Writing Romance*. Take my course *Write Naked*. Or buy any book or course that will give you a little more time to delay writing.

You're welcome.

Okay, fine, you don't have to do step #8, I just threw that in there for a quickie lesson on marketing and pimping yourself out in an uncomfortable fashion.

You're welcome.

Chapter Twenty-Two

How to Write a Book in 30 Days.... (Kind of)

It's been a hell of a year.

I knew back in January it'd be a challenge. I'd decided to take on more travel than I've had before. I was honored to be invited as a keynote speaker and teach a masterclass, and then there were some conferences I needed to attend, including Paris (because who says NO to a signing in Paris?!) and I also needed to write books.

A lot of books. Again, I didn't plan it because sometimes things happen that you need to jump on with contracts – but when 2019 unfolded I realized I needed to write five books in a year that I wasn't around much.

Good thing I love a challenge.

It went much better than I expected. The first three books I churned out had some ups and downs. At one point, I went into panic mode about my first women's fiction novel, but it ended up being a gift and a book I'm so excited about –I'm counting down the days to the release.

But what happened to me probably happens to many other writers who are writing full time and suddenly find their work schedule/family life/travel life intercepts and explodes. We look up one normal, every-day morning, and realize our book is due in thirty days.

One month to write a book.

In some households, this is called NANOWRIMO. For those who are not familiar with the term, it's National Novel Writing Month which is always held in November and encourages writers and anyone who dreams of writing a book to write it in thirty days. Balls to the wall type of guerilla writing. (I talked about this in a previous chapter.)

Now, I like to be able to choose to participate in this program, but this month, I'm forced into it. Because I woke up on October 14th and started my brand-new book, realizing it must be delivered in thirty days.

How shall I do this?

I will explain how, and teach you how to do it, too.

Kind of.

First off, anyone can write a book in thirty days. The problem is the type of book you write. We've all seen The Shining, and we can just type All Work and No Play Makes Jen a Dull Girl over and over and call it a book. I'm talking about a book with a plot, strong characters, a growth ARC, an interesting setting, with some type of theme, great banter, sexual tension and the all-important emotion.

No problem.

Now, I would recommend a few things to start.

One—make it a second or third book in a series. The first one is too hard – you're setting up an entire world and arc of additional books and need more time to do it justice. But with second and third in series, you pretty much know the characters you are going to write, and you are familiar with the world. You can even lean on your first couple to give you some confidence, reminding yourself you did this once and they ended up great and readers loved them.

Writers need to take props anywhere they can.

Second, writing a book in thirty days works much better for seasoned writers. Let's be honest, a newbie is still learning, and putting pressure to write a decent book in thirty days is too much. You need time to learn the craft well, and though there's nothing wrong putting out a first draft, you shouldn't be pressuring yourself to actually make it decent for public consumption at this point. You have much more work to do. Take the time and do it, but commit to getting your initial draft on paper – that will be a great starting point.

Now, with these two caveats in mind, let's move forward.

I started by sketching out a few paragraphs about the characters. Physical attributes, hopes and dreams, some fears, their goals and motivations, etc. Then I bullet pointed some big scenes or turning points that got my juices flowing. Sketched in the greyish type black moment I thought could happen. This is very rough outlining and can veer off the path quickly – this is the kind of outlining I like. I need the surprises to keep me writing along the way. If you're a plotter, you may want to take more time to plot it out but if you have only thirty days to write, this isn't your main goal. Plotters will need to start earlier!

Then, I look at my month and I take out days where big activities are happening, or appointments, or holidays. I try to be realistic about when I can expect to write. Sometimes I give myself a day off on the weekend. Sometimes, I estimate 2-3K per day instead of 5-6K. You need to be ruthless and honest looking at your month but also be balanced. If you're gonna get all ruthless on your ass and pretend you need no down time, you're probably going to stumble. By giving myself some time off with permission, I escape the dreaded funnel where I'm sinking fast and blame it all on that hour my husband's car broke down and I had to drive across town to pick him up and missed a good 2K of words.

At the end of this, your book must total your word count. If your contract says 70K I go with that. If it says 100K I feel very sorry for you. Hopefully, it's more like 50K which is a more reasonable amount to push in one month.

I like to undershoot for a first draft so I don't freak out my Muse.

Next? Write. Write to your schedule. Write no matter what surprises pops up along the way—including a brand new season of your favorite show on Netflix. Practice saying no to things. No to cooking. No to favors. No to going out to dinner with friends for a three hour fun night. No to laundry. No to the kids. One month of no to anything but the writing – which includes your tight social media schedule, those extra cute posts on IG, blogging, promo work, FB ads, etc.

Just say yes to writing.

There will be many times you want to die or scrub toilets rather than see the blank page. If you're a writer who needs to write in logical order and are blocked, you may need to jump around and write a scene that's more interesting. You may need to do things you thought you'd never do before. You may need to change POV's in a scene. You may need to write really stupid scenes just to keep going and get momentum. Your main primary focus is motion.

An object in motion has momentum. More writing begets more writing, not the opposite. It becomes a habit ingrained in the core of who you are, a fingerprint on the keyboard, a constant whispering in your ear that says more, more, more.

Write messy. Write raw. Write honest.

Now, the most important thing moving forward after this mess of a draft is to rely on your editor.

A good editor saves me. My editor is pure gold. As I write the draft, I will put in XXX (some put in TK) where I'd normally need to do research, but I don't want to take the time to lose momentum. Also, I know where scenes are weak and I will put it in there as a red flag for the editor to take a look at.

I will give my editor my own notes on what troubles me on the book. I will ask for help in suggesting a better ending, or black moment. I use my editor because I hired her and she's excellent at her job.

Give her a job to do.

While she's working on that, I begin my research that I left open. I fill in blanks. I tweak things I suddenly understand because I finished the book. I'm clearer and know how to fix shit.

What comes back is suddenly a form you can work on and shape into a good book. Now, you know the characters. You can go back and layer. Make it stronger. Tighten.

The next round is faster –you're getting closer— and if you're breathing this book, you can get a quick turnaround again for the final third draft.

That's the one that goes to copyedits.

So, are you really writing a book in thirty days?

No. More like 45 if you include your edits.

I bet you're asking if I'm afraid the book will be weaker than my others because I rushed it.

The answer?

No, I'm not. I know a good book when I write one —whether it's fast or slow. The fast ones are like immersing myself so deep, I don't see or hear anyone else but my characters. It's harder to live with me during those books because I'm not really here. I'm in the book. I dream about it. I have conversations in my head with the characters rather than my family. It drives me forward –the momentum—but it's still good stuff.

I'm able to do this and know it's good because I have forty books behind me. My Muse and my subconscious take over and I can let them. I couldn't have written a book that fast when I had only ten books to my name. It would have been sloppy. But with so many hundreds of hours logged in from writing (I've been writing book after book since I was 12 years old) my professional instinct and knowledge kicks in and helps level up.

My job is to trust that instinct and let go. Not fight it. Not fight my process, but surrender. Like turning on a faucet, I let the water flow like creative energy and go for the ride. That's how my best work develops.

Now, I'd rather choose to write a book in three months, it's much more comfortable for me. I can take my time and play. Layer. Breathe. But once in a while, this needs to be done, and I rise to the challenge.

For everyone out there pursuing their dream of writing a book – you can do it. Go big. Go deep. Write every day. Push harder than you think you can handle. Say no.

And remember, this is a choice. Another choice was to ask for a deadline extension. I've done this before. Writing a book in thirty days is a lot to take on, but doable if your expectations match your reality.

Chapter Twenty-Three

Five Top Reasons Frozen 2 Illustrates How to Write a Better Book

I just watched *Frozen 2* with my boys this past weekend.

I laughed. I cried. I swooned. I sighed. And I realized I loved this sequel better than the first.

I went with my husband, sister-in-law, and my two boys. They all disagreed with me and said the first one was a lot better. More lighthearted. Funnier. Easier to watch.

I tried to argue, then realized why I was so passionate about this sequel.

I was a romance writer. And the geniuses at Disney did something that the movies haven't been able to do yet. They created all the elements that I look for in a great book.

So, let's break it down. If you haven't seen the movie stop right here.

THERE ARE SPOILERS!

For others still with me, let's have fun with our analysis.

Kristoff was the type of romance hero readers adore.

Oh, Kristoff, how did I not realize your true potential and power? Is it because it was hidden in Frozen and with the new installment you were finally able to shine without competition? This is a hero who's comfortable enough in his own skin to let his woman shine and go on her own adventures. He is not afraid of supporting her and being at her side—and not desperately trying to prove how great he is as a leader. He doesn't try to fix her problems.

The best part of Kristoff? He's in touch with his feelings and has no problem expressing them. Oh, sure, he's bumbling and awkward when trying to propose, but when it comes time to just tell the truth, he does. He keeps it simple but real. When

Write Free

Anna leaves him to go on a quest with her sister, he's out of sorts. He worries if he'd be enough for her. He wonders if he loves her more than she does him. This is all a natural part of loving someone – dealing with doubts and getting to the other side without losing your shit and damaging your relationship. Kristoff launches into a ballad that reminded me of those old eighties videos where men had no trouble singing large and loud about their feelings and I loved every second.

And when Anna returned and needed help the most, he swept in to do his part but never tried to take over.

Best line in the movie: "My love is not fragile." I wept with gratitude. This is what we want our heroes to be.

When bad things happen, we are sometimes overwhelmed and stuck in fear. But the characters we write about move forward, in spite of obstacles.

When Anna loses everyone she holds dear, she collapses into a state of panic and deep grief we've have experienced. Lying in the cave, alone, it seems easier to give up. Why go on? But she finds the strength to move forward, and it comes by just concentrating on the next step. The next step in a long path ahead that can feel insurmountable. That one step eventually leads to another. It may be all you can do – but it is enough for now.

In Anne Lamott's words: "Bird by bird."

This scene is a reminder to all that we will experience terrible burden and tragedy in this life, and some will not get the happy ever after ending we imagined, but by taking a step forward, we have already beaten the odds.

Her song was inspiring and the type of traits I want my stories to resonate with.

Sometimes, we need to sacrifice something we love in order for the greater good.

When Anna realized her beloved city had been protected by lies and hate, she needed to make a decision to sacrifice it for the greater good. We make sacrifices every day with this in mind – for our children, for productivity, for happiness. It never gets easier but with practice, we are able to do it with better intention. Sometimes, we get lucky and get to keep both, like in Anna's case.

Sometimes, we have to let one go and we don't get it back.

This is a theme of life and love that is worth exploring in our books and characters. It is theme. By digging deep into these concepts, we get a richer story.

Everyone has their strengths.

Elsa has magical powers that Anna doesn't. And as angry as Anna is to be left behind, and feel powerless at not being able to protect her sister, Elsa needs to use her magic on her own and not be worried about putting Anna in danger. It's a tough choice but one she commits to whole heartedly. Some may question it, but I believe this choice is a part of knowing what strengths you have and do not.

Anna ends up saving Elsa, but Elsa uses her powers to give Anna the information she needs in order to save her. It's a partnership – both bringing their own assets. It works in family and relationships. Kristoff's strength is allowing Anna to use her full power without worrying if it will upset the male/female balance. He blooms in his support role, which is just as important as a main role. How often we forget that the ones on the sidelines and behind the stage are just as important, even though the audience doesn't know they exist?

Secondary characters are just as important as primary.

Oh, Olaf. How I adore him. His friendship and humor evolved in this movie, and became even more than the first. When we lost him, I cried, because he was no regular secondary character, written into the story for a few laughs and distractions. He was part of the family. His words held deep meaning: "water has memory." He's grown up in this sequel, and I loved every moment of his screen time. Even his comedy was sharper: "I don't even know a Samantha!"

It's a reminder to flesh out our secondary characters and give them depth. Don't be cliché. Don't be shallow. Do the work as a writer to make them interesting and give the reader motivation to want more.

That's it.

Chapter Twenty-Four

Why Editors are Critical to Writing a Great Book

THERE ARE a few things people think of when they hear the term editor.

Deadlines.

A smart person dressed in a business suit with glasses who reads manuscripts all day.

A mysterious figure who takes you to lunch, and decides whether or not she likes your next book pitch and whether to shower you with money or make you starve.

A terrifying presence who can make you cry with one ruthless phrase written in the sidelines of your manuscript. For example: This Sucks.

I've held these images in my head when I was a young writer making my way up the ranks. Now, I look at editors with a completely different vision.

These are the things I now see:

A person who's frustrated, yet tries to remain calm when arguing critical points/changes with an author.

A person who not only needs to balance the story ARCS and details, but be true to the author's voice and vision, while always keeping the reader in mind. In other words, a proficient juggler.

A person who knows every hidden author secret. Like an author's favorite words used over, and over, and over…and over… Or the tendencies to use a phrase so much, it becomes overkill and said editor would like to poke her eyes out with a stick.

A person who must deal with an author's insistence that a reader will "get it" and there's no need to tweak the scene to be clearer.

How about patiently suffering through an author's secret passions for certain television shows, or products that is snuck into every book –Hello, Game of Thrones that is now officially over! Hello baby Yoda who will now be mentioned in the next four books before the trend fades away?

This person needs to ask hard questions that an author doesn't care about when being creative. Such as when the hero throws the heroine on the desk and rips off her clothes and he's her boss and she's an intern – does this scream #METOO movement?

She must ask if your beloved hero is too much of an asshole to deal with. Or if the heroine is too wishy washy and will piss off your audience.

She is paid to whip your ass when you are lazy. I cannot tell you how many times I was exhausted and irritated with a manuscript and stuck something in there because I didn't care anymore, never thinking that the editor will actually question me about such a tiny little thing.

But she did. Every. Single. Time.

And yeah, it's annoying Every. Single. Time.

Later, reading my completed book, I'm so damn happy she was mean to me.

Bottom line? Editors are critical to getting a book from rough draft to polished perfection. It is the editor who truly sees the diamond in the rough, and works tirelessly to polish until the layers of the story is revealed and told in the best way possible.

You see, my peeps, writing a book starts with you. It's a story. It belongs to you. It is your precious. But an editor's job is to strip it down and bring the light into the darkness, to question, and assess, and judge. She is a cheerleader, a therapist, a grammarian, a teacher.

She is a writer's best friend.

Some books are gifts. Some are hell on earth. I've gotten both and learn to appreciate it all—even the books in between.

I think one of the things I remember most about my editor is during the time when my father died. I'd given myself a period off from writing, but I had to get back to it at some point. I remember every day facing that page and needing 2K. It was torturous and painful. Sometimes I'd be in my office till ten pm at night getting those words.

There were many revisions because the first draft was rough. My editor hand held me through each re-write, pushing me closer to the finish line, and though my emotions were so raw I had trouble truly seeing the whole of the book, she did. It took

4-5 rewrites to get the story the way I'd originally imagined it. I'm so grateful for her help and vision.

Is it wrong that every time I see that book cover I still shudder? Yet, it's one of my most emotionally driven stories once I got the other side.

Writers need to learn the best way to work with editors. It's a process and a journey. You learn about each other's hot buttons, likes and dislikes, and what is the best for the book.

A bad editor can make the process an ordeal and have you question your talent and your voice.

A good editor can take your writing to the next level without having you "sell" out.

I'm in re-writes now. For the next few weeks, I'll be polishing to get to the gold, and each time it's both exciting and nerve-wracking for me. Then it will be time to let the book out into the world, where it no longer belongs to me.

But for a little while longer, the book belongs to both of us.

Chapter Twenty-Five

The Power of a Reset

I have to reset every day.

Just because I have a great writing day does not mean it will carry over to the next.

I have to start all over again, from scratch, even if I'm in the middle of a book. Even if I read the paragraph before. Even if I'm brimming with ideas. It's still a brand-new moment I have to show up for in order to continue my story.

It's good news and bad news.

Good because if you have a bad day, you get to start all over again.

Bad, because if you have a productive day, the next one may suck.

It shows the importance and absolute crucial obligation to remain patient. I laugh at people who think this career is exciting, different, thrilling, or fascinating. Okay – sometimes it is. At the best of times, and maybe a few weeks out of the year.

Mostly, it's a boring, tedious career. Because every day you show up and sit. And wait. And tinker. And try. And sometimes you get the ride of a lifetime, but then it stops for dinner, or to pick up the kids, or let the dog out, and you start all over again. You sit back down at the desk and re-start the same shit.

But along the way, something amazing occurs.

The showing up and writing through it all gives us a special and unique gift. The gift to know oneself on the very deepest of levels. It is a meditation of mind and heart and soul. We can never hide from ourselves because we are always putting it on the page, or wrestling it from the deepest caves of our minds, and spilling our secrets.

How damn cool is that?

But to get there, you need patience. You need to wait.

Wait for the Muse; wait for the words; wait for the ideas. Wait for a sentence. Wait for an edit. Wait to finally tie in all the loose threads of your story so it makes sense. Wait for the theme to reveal or a character to finally make sense to you.

Sit…and wait.

Sit…and work.

Sit…and be. Over and over. Day after day.

And that is how you create your greatest work. Your masterpieces. Your final book version that has been dusted off after years of architectural digging and revealed to the world. Don't let anyone ever tell you different—there is no failure in producing art. Ever. There is only failure by giving up. In believing it didn't matter.

Of course, we must do it again. Each time you learn. Get better. Find out more about yourself. Face new fears.

That's our job as writers. That's our gift.

Don't underestimate the power or undervalue the work.

Don't get an ego from it, either. Because the moment you are on top of the world and feeling like God, the next you are scum under someone's shoe and related to an amoeba. Being humble does not mean discarding the importance of creative work. It means you are serving the work—you are open to new ideas without judgement or the rational mind trying to shove you into a category or pin a label on you.

Start every day with intention; purpose; and honor.

Because you are a writer.

Chapter Twenty-Six

The Writing of Fiction by Edith Wharton

THE IDEA of high concept was addressed in Edith Wharton's book, *The Writing of Fiction*, which just came into the public domain.

This is what she says:

First, ask: What judgment on life does the story contain for me?

Quote: "A good subject, then, must contain in itself something that sheds a light on our moral experience."

I've been pondering this question lately as I'm ready to begin my next book. One of the biggest questions asked today from agents or publishers or editors revolves around high concept.

What's the hook? What's the driving question/theme that will demand readers buy this book? What will stand out the most in this overcrowded market?

When you're a writer excited to create and build on a seed to a developing story, this could either be a challenge and motivator, or an energy suck and negative force. Many writers feel their way through the first draft and may not even have figured out this question yet. But in order to pitch a three-book series; you need to have this figured out beforehand.

How can you do it? Especially when Wharton drives home the fact that everyone sees a hook or theme differently, depending on their viewpoint?

I think, therefore, publishers/agents look for common place themes that fall across wider categories. Something that can resonate with most people in broader terms, yet contain elements of excitement to drive them to read the blurb or purchase.

But how do we go about creating those high concept ideas that will resonate in our stories?

I believe as a career author, it's important to focus on elements that drive your own curiosity and that warrant a deeper explanation. For instance, with my book, *Our Italian Summer*, I was fascinated with digging into the dynamics of mothers and daughters. My hook was based on a multi-generational tale of mothers and daughters set against the backdrop of Italy because it allowed me to follow my own goal of the story—unveiling hidden truths and exploring how roles may limit us—but the setting and dual romances offered an interesting hook for a publisher to want to buy.

Go back to Wharton's eternal question when asking yourself if this is the story you need to tell.

What will shed light on your moral experience?

What judgment on life does your story contain?

Those are the ultimate questions. What seeds will you plant to get there?

I am consistently telling writers this is a highly individualized process and journey because we are all unique individuals. I cannot write like you do. I do not see the world the same. This is the beauty of our career – the same story told over and over can be different each time.

If you're a trope driven writer, strip away the

Write Free

mechanics and figure out what judgment will your story contain?

All of this traces back to the all-eternal growth ARC of our characters. Where they begin is not where they will end up. They must grow and change for a satisfying story.

Then, add theme. An overall idea of what you want to explore with all of your characters. Forgiveness? Second chances? What does home mean to you? Am I truly worthy of love? It's a mad, crazy world?

The final piece will answer Wharton's question. It will be an imprint of how YOU saw these characters—your telling of this story—your visual of the world.

Don't be afraid of it. Be unapologetic.

You owe it to your readers.

You owe it to yourself.

Chapter Twenty-Seven

The Power of Story

> "Story doesn't allow us to escape reality but navigate reality." – Lisa Cron, *Story Genius*

I'VE BEEN THINKING about this quote lately as I navigate my life and my writing. I remember back in the day, critics would warn women about the dangers of romance novels, citing how we will forget it's fiction, and believe some dashing, romantic pirate will steal us away from our lives of boredom and give us a happily ever after.

That still pisses me off.

Even before I heard the well thought out and rational arguments, I remember thinking it was bullshit because when I read Stephen King or Sidney Sheldon or even Jackie Collins, I didn't necessarily believe monsters were under my bed or I'd turn into a jewel thief or become a sexy mogul of a hotel empire with men dropping at my feet.

I mean, I WISH.

But story is such a powerful vehicle for people to heal fragments inside themselves and realize we are not alone. That to be human is to love, hurt, hope, fear, and dream mightily. It pushes us to the edge and then sometimes over. It saves us the same exact time it destroys us. Within the pages of books read, and the stories I craft, I'm consistently looking for that element to tie everything together, so when the last page is finished, someone will not only feel more connected, but a bit changed. It offers a new viewpoint – a lens into the world no one else may see except me.

That's powerful stuff. It's the stuff of legends and magic and we can't forget it during the endless tedious hours of editing line by line, and feeling frustrated and blocked by the Muse who taunts us.

The hours put in gets us to the magic. There's no mysterious portal we get to step through in order to reach the end of a well written book. It's mostly blood, sweat and tears, but when we hold it in our hand, the cover glossy, the pages clean and crisp and smelling of sweet paper, our name in raised font scrolled in brilliant color—it's all worth it.

When I'm in the weeds, I go back to the heart and soul of what I'm creating which is built on emotion and being essentially human. Flawed. Yes, grammar, and plot, and theme, and well-crafted dialogue is needed to bring it all together, but the core is always the guts, the messy stuff, and as Lisa Cron teaches, the story. The more we practice and write, the easier we can recognize when we're there and learn how to let go.

I just wrote THE END on my forty ninth book, which means I will begin writing my 50th book in August.

This doesn't count the 8 books I wrote that will never see the light of day in during my learning process. The books under my bed helped shape me into the writer I am today.

Looking back, I never thought about how many books I'd eventually write. I thought about the dreams and glory; the publications and book clubs that would want me; the endless readers begging for my next series installment.

Write Free

One page turned into one chapter. One chapter turned into one book. One book turned into many.

But if I was focused on my fiftieth book, I don't think I would've written my first. Eyes on our own paper, right? No comparing or judging. After all, writers travel alone. There's no need to yank anyone else on our path so we can torture ourselves on everything we are not.

Not famous.

Not rich.

Not well-known.

Not a bestseller.

So, we need to remember one word is good Then a paragraph. A chapter.

A book may lead to another. And another.

Eventually, we look back at where we started, like a college graduate watches as the new kindergarten children step off the yellow bus and begin their school path.

Then they graduate. Get a job. Create a life on their own.

We need to begin somewhere so let's not rush the process.

I've done a lot of writing. And a hell of a lot of stories that guided my way.

I wouldn't have it any other way.

Chapter Twenty-Eight

Lessons in Solitude

I WAS READING Michael Ventura's brilliant piece, "The Talent of the Room", and began thinking about the power of solitude.

In a world where everything moves so fast, from a tap to like an IG post, to a swipe left to show interest in a person, to busy talk shows crammed with opinions in rapidly rising voices as if the loudest can still win the argument, our world is created for noise.

After the pandemic hit, and people began to quarantine, the notion of solitude was a new element many struggled with. They went from offices bustling with activity to a computer at home in their office. Expensive lunches making big deals morphed into static emails. And weekends full of social commitments such as dinners and festivals and parties slowed to nothing.

Depression hit. Boredom. Relationships were tested. And as the world slowed to silence, some of us began to embrace this mysterious quality that we match to Buddhist monks or priests or people we like to term hermits.

Solitude.

In order to be a successful writer, we learn to thrive in solitude. But I've also learned this past year in my discovery of meditation, that within the quiet is so much more. There are answers that have been blocked by the endless voices of the mind, consistently planning, critiquing, pushing, and achieving.

I've begun to learn that by sitting in silence, I do more soul work than I do when I'm busy. Beyond the thoughts is more than quiet, it's a way to figure out what's important and what's not. Who I am. What I want to say.

It's been a gift I want to train, so even if it's for 3 minutes where I focus on my breath, or gently stop my scurrying mind from telling me I suck, I love peeking into the portal of endless opportunity and amazing stories lurking beneath. I feel like a child giggling in a hidden closet while my parents stomp around looking for me so I can get back to chores.

I like who I'm finding there. She's certainly not perfect, and has issues, and most of the time she's a big fat mess, but that's okay too. I don't write about perfect characters either, because I can't relate.

Within imperfection and mess is the good stuff. That's what you find when you sit alone in a room to write, or when you sit in silence with yourself for those precious three minutes.

There's no special training, either. Sure, there's a bunch of courses and mediations you can download or YouTube videos to follow, but all you really need to do is pause, breathe, and pay attention to your body.

The thoughts will chase themselves as they are used to. I don't try to stop them—the process is to gently and firmly dis-attach and return to the breath. Maybe you do it for a minute. Maybe three.

Do it when you feel overwhelmed or stressed. Do it when you remember. Do it before you open your manuscript. It's a way to slow things down and re-connect.

No chanting or instruction is needed unless you want it.

Do you know what I've found from the practice?

I'm beginning to like it there.

Chapter Twenty-Nine

The Very First Love Story

We always remember our first, right?

First kiss, first love, first pet, first tragedy? It's different from naming our favorite. The first is sometimes wonderful, sometimes painful, but always poignant.

When people ask me about when I first started writing, I always refer to the very first book I wrote when I was twelve years old. It was a young adult romance based on the shy, smart girl no one noticed and the bad ass popular kid from the wrong side of the tracks. The book was called Challenges of the Heart. I used everything about my life to write it, drawing from personal experiences, and using real life friends as my secondary characters. Every moment I wrote that story I remember pure joy.

This was before I knew too much about craft, or worried about publishing, or got bogged down by details. My soul just soared because I was caught up in the beauty of the story, the romance between the characters and their rocky journey toward love.

My mother used to yell at me to put my notebook down. I drifted off in school most days, thinking about my book and I couldn't wait to get back to it. Nothing else mattered, I was caught in the helpless spell of creating a romance that would change two people forever – and in my world, they were very, very real. They spoke to me, changed me, supported me. They made me brave and helped me reach for my dreams. They were my very first characters, and I still have that notebook today—worn, battered, faded. I look at my childish script and I hold my first real book in my hand. The first book I ever wrote and believed in. And yes, it brings me both joy and a sadness, when I think about that young girl who was so passionate about life, and how many times she was bent along the way, but never broken.

That's what romance novels do to us. They help us not break. They take us away from the pain of life for a few precious hours, and give us hope, peace, and some happiness. Oh, and so much joy.

Do romance novels change the world? Will they ever be touted as magnificent masterpieces, and pushed in our schools to be read, or held up in the lofty NY Times Book reviews?

Probably not.

But I believe romance novels change one woman at a time. A few hours of joy must negate many hours of pain, right?

My memory is getting foggier as I age, but damned if I still can remember every detail of reading certain romance books that transported me into another time and dimension. Books from my keeper shelf that I re-read and experience the same type of emotion years later.

I like to think back to my very firsts. I remember a reader telling me my book, *The Marriage Bargain*, got her to love reading again. She said my book was a portal to another world.

I cling to that reminder when things get hard. I made a difference.

With a romance novel.

Is there a romance book that changed your life? Or one you remember so clearly, because you read it during an important part in your life?

Take some time, close your eyes, and remember. Journal. Reminding ourselves of such joy and power help us re-commit to our dreams to do the same for someone else out there.

Chapter Thirty

The Element of Passion

READERS USE the adjective passionate to describe romance novels in various ways. A hot sex scene, sizzling sexual tension, a feisty argument – all of these elements combined helps readers experience passion with our characters, which is key to the book.

But there are other ways of bringing passion to a reader. In my latest book, *Unbreak my Heart*, I use music and food to weave a sensual feast of taste and sound, and layer the story with other elements to increase the overall effect of the story.

Let's look at music. My heroine adores the opera. Sounds stuffy to some? Actually, I use the lush music and story of both La Traviata and Pagliacci to heighten the sexual tension and lure the reader into another world, describing the way it feels when they are seated at the Metropolitan, watching the dramatic story on stage unfold which mirrors what my hero and heroine are also going through.

I love a story where the author teaches me about an art I don't know too much about, or brings me into certain passions the characters have, whether it be a hobby or a career. I weave the opera theme carefully throughout the structure to keep balance and enhance my characters.

How about food? Ah, the texture and scents and flavors of food in an Italian kitchen is a great way to grab the reader and ground them in the setting. When my heroine is eating what the kitchen prepares, describing the experience will hopefully make a reader hungry. Bringing the act of cooking and preparing food into the love story is a great tool to heighten the communication and show deeper facets of the characters.

For example, my hero loses a waiter at a critical time and needs the heroine's help. When she dons her apron and dives headlong into the kitchen, a passion for quality and service comes out, and the characters bond on a new level. Of course, this all ends up in a hot scene on top of the bar...but that's another type of passion for another article!

I'm able to make my secondary characters pop in the story by using Frank Sinatra and the Rat Pack to entwine some humor and lighten the mood. My hero's father has his own Italian posse where they speak in Sinatra-isms, drink, play cards, and discuss the Rat Pack. They take these dialogues quite seriously, and even fight to defend their individual opinions. Again, by making this group care about something deeply, a writer can bring a new level of passion to the story that has nothing to do with the physical.

Animals or children is another great way to incorporate passion into a story. What reader doesn't melt when the hero softens his barriers around a child or his beloved dog? Or turning a heroine into an advocate for animal shelters or rescued wildlife is a great way to show her nurturing personality or hint at softer qualities she tries to hide.

When we are passionate about something, the energy leaks and crackles to the page. Readers can feel it and this helps lure them into the story world.

What type of passionate elements do you enjoy in your stories? Music, movies, art, cooking, wine, food, animals? How can you integrate them into the seams of your story?

Chapter Thirty-One

Write What You Know...and Don't

WRITE What you Know

No one else out there knows what you know. I'm not talking about facts you can find on the Internet. I'm talking about personal experiences that you've been through.

I have always had a rocky relationship with my father. He was an alcoholic, left when I was fifteen, and I didn't see him for two years because he disappeared so he wouldn't have to pay child support. I met him again at a Dunkin Donuts when he was driving a cab, standing in line for coffee.

Slowly, we rebuilt a relationship because I made a rational decision, he was the only father I had, and it was up to me to decide what type of relationship we'd have. When I was twenty-five, he went to rehab for the fifth time and stayed clean. He never drank again. He rebuilt a foundation and over the years, we became close, though I always knew his limitations.

When he died, a lot of stuff came up. Tons of emotions and mess that was a tangle I needed to sort out. I've written many stories about alcoholic fathers, or parental relationships that were broken and bad, exploring how each of the characters figured it out.

You see, everyone reacts differently. One character who started as an alcoholic can keep drinking, or choose to be a better person, or spend his life filled with hate and resentment that he didn't get a fair shake. The character being hurt can decide to walk away with no further contact; try to repair the relationship; forgive; or not.

This is my stuff. I took my experiences and emotions and spun it to the page for endless exploration in my stories.

Write What you Don't Know

Write Free

When I was in Italy with my mom, niece and godmother, I outlined an ambitious women's fiction book about three generations of women whose relationships were fragmented and went to Italy to heal. I had an idea of the characters I wanted to write. In my head, this was a big romp of travel and adventures and growth. An unveiling of relationships between each woman.

The proposal stayed in my computer for five years before I was able to sell it. When I did, I went into a deep panic.

Sure, I'd gone to Italy a few times, but I didn't live there. I didn't know the ins and outs. I had to expertly write about an eighteen-year-old, a seventy-year-old, and a forty-year-old in their respective POVs. I had to describe an Italian tour from the inside out. I had to write about a ton of secondary characters.

I was terrified I'd made a mistake claiming I could write this book.

There is no way I can express the hard work and despair I felt during this book. I believed I was failing on every level. The voices that told me I couldn't write a real big women's fiction novel because I sucked and was never good enough.

I faked myself out before I even tried to write a word.

A good friend finally got me out of the pit of hell and told me, "You're trying too hard to write a different type of book. But what you need to do is be you and write the book the way you feel comfortable. Don't try to be someone you're not. Write the story from the place that you live and are comfortable. Just write a Jennifer Probst book."

Lightbulb moment.

I took her advice and everything changed. By giving myself permission to simply write my book, and not muddle my brain with thoughts of what a good women's fic book should do, I went back to the story. I began to trust myself again. And I wrote the rest of the book on fire.

Springboard on what you do know but don't be afraid to reach for the stars and be uncomfortable writing something you don't.

We need both in our books.

Chapter Thirty-Two

Chasing The Story

SOMETIMES, I forget that writing is like life. You can have clear goals, focus on the finish line, and do the work nonstop to get there. But many times, the end is just out of reach—like the treasure keeps tauntingly moving a few steps ahead of you until you wonder:

Was this a good idea in the first place?

Is this not meant to be?

Will I ever really get there?

I've pondered these questions through books I wondered if I hadn't been meant to write; projects that seemed like a great idea at the time but then blew up; and personal goals that seemed to dissipate in the harsh morning light.

Most of the time, I get there, though. The funny thing?

Many times, the end was not what I imagined it to be.

I found an old folder with some of my rough notes sketched out for the development of some books I'd written. After leafing through them, I was amazed at how much changed from the original story concept. I've always been a pantser—I figure out the story as I go along—but I do have firm ideas of character, rough plot, or specific scenes I'm excited to write.

Would it have been a better book if I'd stuck with the plan?

Maybe. Maybe not. And who cares at this point? The book is out in the world and I can say I'm damn proud of every book I put out there. Each one was lovingly crafted and contains my blood, sweat and tears.

Next time, I'd like to be more graceful in accepting the end is not what I planned. Most times, the road branches off to bigger roads and we find out

Write Free

later, they were all intermingled the entire time. You cannot break off one and get the same result years later.

Story is like that. An idea nugget grows and shoves us off in different directions. I think many writers freeze and don't even try to finish the book because of all the overwhelming choices—and our stubborn refusal to accept the end may be different. This doesn't mean plotters are wrong to be frustrated if the book isn't getting written as planned. It's more of a concept that if we allow ourselves to experience the surprises along the way, we may find the end is better than what could have even imagined.

The seeds have always been planted. The whisper in your ear, teasing you forward.

But it takes a bit of faith. Trust. Belief in creativity and our ability to get there.

I think with the harshness of the world lately; all the challenges and toxic culture and raw emotions pouring forth; it would be nice to take a gentler approach to our writing. To be more open to possibilities and surprising outcomes.

I'm trying to do this more in my writing right now, and my life. I like the way it's turning out.

My achiever mode is sometimes a bit frustrated, but I'm reminding myself going slower and taking the long path doesn't mean we're not getting to the end.

We're just taking a more leisurely, scenic route. And if we smell the flowers and listen to the creak of branches under out feet and experience the hot sting of the sun on our face along the way?

Well, wasn't it more pleasant? Who cares if it took longer? I enjoyed the journey more. How could that be wrong?

We're still chasing the story. Our stories.

But we're chasing them with more joy.

Chapter Thirty-Three

Blue Lamborghini

The car was a smooth, slick blue,

And it roared down the endless route.

Hands clasped around the wheel ready to steer,

Feet on the pedal, shifting the gear.

It hummed in beauty as the roof opened,

Oh, a never-ending road, this car was my token.

It burned rubber across the mountainside,

The harsh smell of it only intensified.

Man, I love this blue Lamborghini,

This car to me was as special as a lamp with a genie.

The color was bluer than the ocean,

And people stared at it as we went by in slow motion.

The wheels skidded once we arrived at our stop,

My feet walking away from it, as it sat there on the blacktop.

Because once I buy the car, the trip will never end!

My son wrote this poem. I've been thinking about it a lot.

He said he always thought poetry sucked until his teacher forced them to write one. Afterward, he told me he realized he liked the way he could express things in imagery and have fun with rhyme. He enjoyed the challenge it posed.

I wrote poetry when I was young. Most of it was bad, but my mom still keeps the notebook with my treasured poems written about my life, which mostly revolved around books and my dog. It was important to me, then. I was learning how to express myself. Figuring out what I liked, what I didn't, and what was interesting enough for me to write about. Experimenting with words and flow.

Write Free

Falling into the process as writers do when we're focused on chasing the story to see how it turns out.

I enjoy the way my son sees the world – driving down the road one day in his slick blue Lamborghini. It reminds me of a writing career – this job we cherish and agonize over and love and hate all in one sloppy lump of emotion.

How good it feels to climb into a new story and start the engine. The easy, smooth speed of the road ahead, hugging the curves, feeling the wind in your hair and elation singing in your blood.

The harsh bumps of false stops and starts. The way people stare at our books and our choices; judge; dispersing reviews and opinions while we drive on by. Some we care about. Some we don't.

The wheels skidding to a halt at the end—our destination reached. Walking away from the story because the ride is finished, but knowing we'll be back again, because for us, it's only one ride in a long line of Lamborghinis—some blue, some yellow, some black, some white.

Our trip is never-ending.

Yeah, sometimes it feels like we're in a 1980 Chevette and praying to make it home before it falls apart.

But most of the time, it's a hot blue Lamborghini and we love it hard; show it off; and wait for the next adventure.

Write your asses off, peeps.

Go take your ride.

Chapter Thirty-Four

Life Lessons from the Dog

I'VE BEEN a bit MIA for a while.

It's all been good stuff. The past two months have been a whirlwind, and when I realized it's been a while since I wrote a decent post, I figured I'd take some time and update everyone.

First, I went to RARE Paris. I learned that the French are not rude, or mad that you can't speak the language. They are actually quite kind and charming and I fell madly in love with the city of love. Now, I know why they call it that. I was lucky enough to stand in the gorgeousness of Notre Dame five days before the fire. I bought a golden set of rosary beads from the gift shop, and I treasure them so much—a reminder of the beauty before the fire ripped through, and I hope they will restore it to the original glory.

I drank champagne every day, all day. This has led me to the firm belief I need to drink it regularly and not save it for a special occasion. It's just too good.

The readers came out in droves and showered me with gifts and love and I am so humbled that my work has been translated into French. How did I get this amazing and blessed life? I try to remind myself of this during the difficult writing times.

My son received confirmation and when I saw him dressed in his suit, taller than me, I was struck by the issue of time and all its complexity. It goes so slow when we're young, and increases with each year to Superman like speed. I want to slow it down, but I can't, so I just remind myself to take time to watch my son's baseball games and track races and help with homework, and take weekends off to be with them.

Then, I went to Texas for Inkers Con and was amazed at the beauty of this conference. The workshops and speakers and authors were so damn talented and I learned a ton. I met new friends and created business relationships and networked. Another lesson learned: get out of your office. It's critical to meet other writers and to experience a conference where ideas are flying and being shared.

You realize you're finally with your people. Writers have issues. We are a little insane. This is why it's important to connect and know we're not alone.

All of this leads up to one of the best decisions made in my household. I have been grieving the loss of my fur baby, Bella. She's been gone for eleven weeks now. It's been three months full of pain and grief.

But now, we decided to adopt a new rescue and she's changed my life.

Her name is Willow. She's eight pounds, and full of love and mischief.

There's just one thing. I forgot that I'm old. I'm not used to babies or puppies. I'm not used to getting up at the crack of dawn to walk her, or being interrupted every 2 hours for playtime or potty breaks. I'm not used to following them around the house to discipline if there's an accident, and seeing a hundred chew toys scattered in every room. She makes me tired. But oh, the lessons I've been reminded of!

Here are a few:

The world is really a beautiful place.

Dear Lord, this puppy is straight from a Disney movie. She is full of joy and wonder when she steps outside. She tries to eat everything, and when the blossoms from the trees fly in the wind, she pounces like a cat and tries to catch them. She sticks her nose in every bush and flower bed and sniffs. She chases bees and butterflies and birds. She follows scents and listens to every sound. She makes friends with chipmunks. She runs with wild abandon and no fear of what's ahead, dying to discover the next surprise. She has reminded me of what it's like to see the world with new eyes, and I'm treasuring every moment, even as I admit I'm tired!

Damn, we're going to make a ton of mistakes.

When she ate the nasty mud splattered thing before I could stop her, she spit it out and seemed to wonder what the hell had she'd been thinking. When she attempts to chew wires and gets disciplined, she's sad. When she thought she could be dominant with a bigger dog and got nipped, she realized she can't bully everyone. It's a constant learning experience, reminding me it's okay to mess up. We're all going to do it, and why are we so damn hard on ourselves when we do? We deserve kindness, especially from ourselves.

We all need play and rest time.

This pup knows how to have fun. Whether it's chasing a ball, tag, or tug of war, she puts her heart and soul into it. When she finally sleeps, she goes into a state I'm jealous of—a comatose, deep relaxation I wonder if I'll see again. I realize when I'm forced to walk or play every two hours, I've forgotten to moan or worry about my interrupted work.

Instead, I simply take a walk with her. Or eat lunch and share. Or steal a nap and snuggle. The beauty of such simple tasks in life sometimes gets overrun in our motivation to reach our goals. To work harder and longer and faster. God knows, I've done it, and succeeded by that philosophy, but I'm also learning there's a time for other things. Once you stop working as hard, you realize your life won't really fall apart. It's all going to be there waiting for you, and maybe, you'll do even better with a break – whatever that break means for you.

There are lessons surrounding us all the time, but the best are learned by the ones we love.

What were some you learned from your dog? Your children? Your partner? Yourself?

Chapter Thirty-Five

Why It's Okay to Blow Things Up

I LOVE *Little House on the Prairie*.

I'm saying it loud and proud. Don't even care if it shows my age or people make fun of me. The show makes me feel cozy, warm, and as if I'm wrapped in a tight blanket. There are terrible tragedies that happen in the show, but it's like a novel for me, where even though awful things will happen, I'm offered hope at the end.

Not like a romance. Those are my guaranteed happy ever afters. But when the credits and familiar theme song begin to play, I know there is possibility and hope for new growth, even through the pain.

During the final season, viewership dropped, and they wrapped up by putting out an epic finale that most people despised. I have a love/hate relationship with the ending, but mostly I kind of love it.

Spoiler alert ahead!

The town is taken over by a railroad mogul, a rich asshole who manipulates the people to trust him, buys the town, and decides to transform it for his business. He pretty much throws out all the main characters and their small businesses and farm. Basically, his intent is to completely destroy Walnut Grove forever.

Awful, right? A great villain. You think they'll find a loophole or a way to save the town, because that's what should happen in a good story.

Nope, not with Little House. Instead, the townspeople band together and decide to blow up Walnut Grove with dynamite.

WTF?

Yes. They decide if they need to lose, the villain shall lose, too. They sacrifice the place they love; their home; but they do it on their terms.

Write Free

No one wins. The town is gone. But damn, when the villain comes riding in and sees his profit completely disappear because of these impulsive, angry people, there's a deep sense of satisfaction.

Yeah, I think. Blow it all up. Take that, bad guy.

What does Little House on the Prairie have to do with writing?

A lot.

I think many writers feel trapped. Trapped with the need to write a marketable book they can sell. Trapped by the limits they believe are in the marketplace. Trapped by needing to go viral on TikTok, or show up everywhere on social media, or sell a certain amount or get enough KU page reads. Trapped by numbers and admin and writer's block.

Trapped by fear.

Because underneath? It's all run by fear. I'm writing this post today because I'm in the thick of fear right now, for a variety of reasons, and I need to make sense of things and calm my mind. Sometimes, it's meditating, or talking to a friend, or sleeping. Sometimes, it's escape. Sometimes, it's writing.

I got to thinking that when there's a crossroads, trust and faith help me the most. A new outlook. Steeping myself in gratitude. Reminding myself I'm exactly where I need to be, and if I keep moving forward, good things will happen.

But sometimes?

You may need to blow things up.

You may need to step away from a genre you've been writing in and building, to do something else. A book that calls you and makes you excited again. A book that's different from what you've been doing.

Maybe you need to blow up your current author brand and create a pen name.

Maybe you need to blow up something that's making you unhealthy and sad. Your job. Your marriage. A toxic friendship. Trying to be good for everyone. Trying to stay in your lane and stay quiet.

Maybe by blowing it all up, you get to start something brand new. A business. A YouTube channel. A painting. A memoir. A course.

I quit cleaning my house years ago and it was the

best money I ever spent, and the most precious time I ever got back.

Maybe you need to stop believing that everyone else is right.

Maybe you need to fire someone. Or quit a social media channel making you sick. Or stop reading the news and read romance novels instead.

Blowing things up doesn't have to be negative. It can be freeing. It can allow new space in your life, even though it's scary as hell.

I'm a big proponent of following things through; of relying on grit and perseverance when things get hard. I still believe it, but now I'm also open to the idea that many things in life may not be good for you.

Maybe it's God or Fate or the universe screaming for you to not go in that direction anymore.

Can't you see it?

Nope. Sometimes we can't. But we can be quiet and listen to our bodies and feel our way through things. Feel if it's right.

I believe the town was very sad about losing their home. I also believe they ended up okay—in new places, with new adventures to experience. Perhaps, they would've never found their true destiny if they'd been able to stay and be safe. Maybe they would've missed their best story.

Blowing things up can be the best decision you ever made.

I'm glad *Little House on the Prairie* reminded me of it today.

Chapter Thirty-Six

What Next? I've Done Everything Perfect but my Book still Failed

BUCKLE UP, buttercups. I'm in the mood to write something raw and vulnerable, in the hope there are others out there my words will either help, support, or soothe.

This career is truly a roller coaster ride. Up, down, sideways, upside down, pause, stop, go. One of the most important pieces of advice is to keep going. Believe in yourself and your stories. Cultivate grit. Keep your head down and focused on you and move forward.

But sometimes, you feel like the universe is lining up for a lightning strike. That perfect opportunity where the world aligns and you sense your book is going to blow up.

I've had this only a handful of times. I go into every book launch with positivity, grace, and the knowledge I gave it my all. It's enough for me to sleep well at night, even with the occasional regret no writer will ever avoid. Once, this belief changed my life. Another time, I made a quiet ripple in an industry that meant a lot to me.

This time? Well, I failed.

What book is it?

Book of the Month.

Peeps, the moment I brainstormed this story I felt the knowledge shimmer that I had something special. Even my bestie who hears about the choices I make in deciding what book to write next said she felt it. "This one is going to be huge!" she said to me excitedly.

And I agreed. Quietly. Inside, where no one could hear. The story was a dream to write. I signed with a publisher I loved and knew would treat me like gold. They poured a ton of money into marketing and I always felt valued. The title was a perfect hook. The cover a dream. The reviews poured in with praise. Influencers posted about it and talked about it. Barnes & Noble made a special Nook edition with bonus content and it hit big on the charts.

Everyone worked so hard, but this felt special. We all chattered in low voices, dug in, and got ready for the explosion.

But—it never came. The book simply never took off. Sales were below average, and not even close to what we all expected. And months later, I'm still sitting here puzzled and confused because it's still one of my faves, and I still believe it has untapped, fantastic potential for growth.

What happened? How did it all quietly die when we were on twenty-four-hour watch? What could I have done differently?

I don't know. I just don't. I had a long talk with my publishers and readers and my content creators. I had great swag! It had the best hook! The spice was delicious! It was funny and emotional!

But the book sank, no matter how many times we put lifejackets on it.

This is a very hard thing to not only accept, but live with. It kind of haunts me, like an ex who I still love and believe we can be each other's besties, but it hurts too much. The timing was off. It's the one who got away.

I'm sure you're waiting to hear what I did. How I made that book take off. How I took the failure with grace and made the best of it.

But I can't, because I'm still stubbornly mourning and determined to give it life. I have another shot. The second book in the series comes out this summer, and it may resurrect *Book of the Month*. It's called *The Reluctant Flirt* and it's so good, guys. I simply love it. So does the team. It's got a great cover. It's a summer story taking place in the Outer Banks.

Once again, I'm hopeful, yet I know I could be disappointed. You can have everything go perfectly but something is misaligned and it's simply not your book's time. Maybe it can come later. You always wait, bring it back out, tinker and see if there's a sale, a tweak, a newsletter, fresh ads, an opportunity for it to pop.

I'm putting my all in to the new book and going big. I have to, or I'll always wonder.

We all need to make hard decisions with our books. There will always be certain ones that never sell. I have a few. I've mourned and done my grieving. You need to move on after a certain amount of time or face the risk of getting stuck. Our minds need to be clear on the road ahead. The next love affair, not the ones in the past.

But like the lottery, every day is a possibility to win. That's what's so cool about being an author. We have all these wonderful children in our nest ready for their big moment. Every piece of content is valuable. That is the one thing I teach over and over and believe in at my core.

Forget about closing.

Always be writing.

For all my peers who loved a book and mourned its failure, I'm sending hugs. But let that not define us. We are not failures because of a failed book. We did nothing wrong. A book not doing well feels personal, but it's separate. Once we put that book into the world, it no longer belongs to us. Therefore, we cannot allow it to define us—neither by success, or failure.

It was simply not our time.

Chapter Thirty-Seven

It's an Inside Job

As we trudge through the depths of February and winter, it can be a great time for reflection.

There are so many projects we dream about doing.

Writing a book. Painting a canvas. Teaching a class. Building a business.

We use calendars and deadlines. We try pushing hard until we're bruised by our own self-criticism and self-flagellation. We dream of being different people who actually succeed and meet goals and get things done.

But what if we are already exactly who we should be? What if we don't need to change the inside at all? What if we learn to make space for our fear and doubts in total acceptance without fighting it?

Remove the resistance and there's no longer anything to fight.

Maybe what is really need is massive action no matter what's lurking inside. We get in our heads and overanalyze—we cite our personality defects and reasons why we are broken.

What if being broken is exactly what we need to be uniquely us? To have what we create be so special because a whole person could never have seen what we see?

Maybe if we start looking at ourselves differently and appreciating all our pieces, we can move forward in a fresh way.

For years, I wondered why I couldn't write books with plenty of time before deadline. I'd try really hard. I'd calculate word count and organize but find myself doing other things; delaying writing; believing I had plenty of time.

We call these people procrastinators. It's a negative term which I believe is misused.

What if we are simply people who work well under the steady pressure of urgency? What if that exact urgency inspires us to move forward, knowing there is now a time frame, and massive action is needed. Thinking is behind us. Worrying is behind us. Analyzing and coming up with a million ways we can fail is behind us.

Because we need to do immediately, and when we are doing, we are not thinking. Our minds take a step back and give us the room to do the work.

I've taken a bunch of workshops and seminars that break down the assholery of our given brain, and what tools we can use to manage it for the good. To help us succeed rather than trying to protect us by imagining endless failures.

I don't yell or criticize myself anymore about waiting too close to deadlines. It gives me a sense of urgent excitement that motivates me to write. When the clock is ticking, I feel alive. I feel driven.

Others may need different stimulations to drive them to action. Find yours. Think about the times when you have completed the things that make you proud to be you. Times that amazed you. Some may be inspired by grit, or their family's needs, or money.

We can do only so much prep work before we need to move.

Write Free

Find your urgency. Find the action.

Move your body and get the energy up. Create a deadline. Put up a preorder or press the record video or write a scene that sucks. Recruit a friend or partner to push. Write down the one action that you will complete today.

Make the time. We all have the time. Choose to use the time to act and not prep, or think, or worry, or wait.

Chapter Thirty-Eight

The Lowest Standard of Performance is Perfection

PERFECTION KILLS ACTION. It is the barrier. Our minds love perfection because it keeps us safe.

Let's make this week full of work that moves the needle forward. Not busy work.

Action work.

Right now, I'm working on constructing a writer's course. It's a project I've wanted to start for almost two years. I have very good excuses for putting it off. Endless deadlines and other work that's more familiar and easier to choose. Fear of getting in front of a camera and being vulnerable. Doubts on how to put it together or if anyone would want to buy it.

It's easy to lean on my need for perfection to deny the real stuff I'm feeling. There is a difference between wanting to put out quality work and the stringent rules of perfectionism.

Perfectionism allows us to hide. Be safe from criticism, rejection, or failure. If we drag it out into the light and examine without fear, we can see this element for what it really is.

Like the child who wails and falls into a tantrum when the puzzle piece doesn't fit. Or the tide of bitterness that washes through us when a dream doesn't meet our reality.

The only way to blast through the barrier is to do. Take a step forward. Push through the discomfort, take a breath, and hit the launch button. Publish the book. Write the first chapter.

This week, I'm writing out a module and getting in front of the camera. It's an action step that will move me closer to my goal. I don't care if I haven't figured out what video editing program to use, or if my makeup sucks, or if mess up when I speak. I have things I'm burning to share and the only thing holding me back is the endless excuses and fear of taking uncomfortable action.

There is a time to think. A time to let intellection grab the reins and back off. To let the Muse take hold and float down the river.

And there's a time to stop research or worrying or delaying and simply do the thing. The action. Even if your heart feels like its beating out of your chest and it's not perfect.

Channel your inner Yoda.

There is no try. There is only do.

Do the thing. Now.

What's one thing you can do today that's action oriented?

Chapter Thirty-Nine

An Intimate Session with Anne Lamott

ONE OF THE writing books I treasure most in my life is, *Bird by Bird*, by Anne Lamott. It was as if I was nodding my head throughout the pages, and felt seen – as a writer and creative. And as a human being with endless flaws.

It's still dog-eared and shelved right behind me. I keep it close for comfort. When I attended A Writing Room virtual retreat, she was the closing keynote. Seeing her beloved face and hearing her speak the words I'd read in my head many times was a beautiful moment. And once again, she proved how well she understood all of us writers.

The most powerful bullet-points from her speech

follows below that I wanted to share while it was still fresh in my mind.

Shitty First Drafts: The book we imagine in our head is never the same when we put it on the page. In our minds, it is a work of art. On the blank page, it is a piece of crap.

Mostly. That is why it's so important to keep the critic voice separate from the writing. Our minds are assholes but their goal is to keep us safe. They try to do this by not letting us fail or be vulnerable to the world. But if we can calmly recognize the voice telling us this whole thing won't work, and allow them their tantrum and then put them to the side, we can get on with the work.

Writing is a living, breathing thing. We tinker and play. We sit in mindful frustration as we try to find the right words or expressions. We layer characters and fix conflict. We worry. We soar.

We need to respect the process and sucking is the first step.

"It doesn't have to be perfect. It just has to start." – Denise Linn

. . .

Writing Consistently:

Lamott says, "Give up NOT writing. I'm most happy when I'm writing. I'm the unhappiest when I'm not."

Yes, we still need to sometimes step away to refill the well, so being in tune to our process and our bodies is important. To live by our gut if it says step out of the office.

But writing is simply something that needs to be learned and grows by writing. Doing it over and over and over. Trying to write in different formats to stretch our abilities and talents. Reading about writing craft. Taking classes on craft. Yes, selling is important but our product is our books.

Sometimes, when we're focused on writing and publishing for money, we may get sidetracked by the longing to write something for ourselves. If I'm on the publishing train for too long, cranking out sellable books, my Muse gets quiet and a bit cranky. Eventually, she shuts down. I know I need to feed her with fresh food; new energy; a new adventure.

This is the time I try to write various blog posts that thrill me, or a short story that I tell myself I will batch up and create an anthology for in the future; or an essay about something big in my life that I want to remember and can share later.

This is the time I take some risks. It's when I began my first serial novel with the RED series and published it in Kindle Vella a year later. I wrote children's books with my boys and nieces one summer. I wrote nonfiction for writers. I fed my Muse even when my mind told me there was no time.

There is always time. We simply need to choose what we want to do with it.

We need to get out of the office to live so we can write bigger.

We need to get out of our writing comfort zone so we can grow and reach bigger heights with our craft.

Trust:

Lamott has a calmness in her voice that settles me immediately. She has built her career on trust. She shared how each book feels like her last; that she still sees herself as an imposter; but by showing up and writing, there is a trust that has been built that is unshakeable.

Write Free

Isn't that a beautiful idea? That we can build our love and trust for ourselves just by showing up to write? That with all the noise out there, people tearing us down or doubting; reviews making us worry; the rush to succeed blurring the actual art of writing—that in the depth there is this quiet trust and love for our own words?

That's the stuff we need to cling to when it gets hard.

As I always say, in the end, it's just you, in a room, alone, with a blank page.

Some people think that sounds scary.

As a writer, that end seems like pure heaven to me.

Chapter Forty

The Art of Immersion

I just returned from an amazing writing conference called Romance Author Mastermind. I was able to give a keynote, and then sit in endless sessions for three full days from the top people in the business. Being surrounded by such greatness and soaking up the new ideas made my brain pop and crackle like the best Rice Krispie cereal!

I also attended a virtual retreat from A Writing Room. Great authors from around the world in all disciplines came to speak, including the amazing Anne Lamott, who is a writing mentor to me. Cheryl Strayed, the author of Wild, gave a ninety-minute presentation. The guest speakers all brought something unique to teach.

This retreat was much quieter than RAM. It was about delving beneath the surface of writing and didn't focus as much on publishing/marketing. We wrote with various prompts and took time to really look at our writing voices with patience. I think this is just as important as making seven figures and the perfect follow up to RAM.

Afterward, I began to think about the process of immersion as a learning tool. I believe writing is a practice that helps us connect with immersion because we become the story we are writing, not just the creator but an active participant.

We are our first reader. We see where we are bored or excited or where the emotional punches of a scene lie. We see all the bruises and scabs but also the awe-inspiring beauty of words told perfectly on the page. It's an act that gets greater with more practice. We are better writers at book twenty than book one.

But immersion isn't just about writing. It's a part of life I love to explore because I think it opens up new doors inside us that remain shut too many times due to fear. Sometimes, doing it once is wonderful, but many don't return to do things a second or third time. Especially if it's scary.

I've gone on a roller coaster once and walked away saying, "Okay, I did it. Never again."

But the times I pushed to go on a second time? It has made all the difference. I had a new perspective because I wasn't terrified any longer. And if I pushed to a third time, I usually ended up loving the experience and getting a high from the feeling.

Immersion is doing something again and again until the fear is gone, or you feel more comfortable being uncomfortable.

We can take foreign languages in school for years, but I spoke more Italian by going to Italy and being dropped in the center of the city for ten days and needing it to navigate.

Same thing with learning a skill. I have many blocks about things I feel I can't do, or won't be good at. Many times, I'll take a course, learn a module, do the lesson once, and then find myself never returning. Which is probably the human mind and that nonstop chattering voice of our inner critic telling us it won't help anyway.

I have to remind myself to go back and do it again, even if I don't want to. Because I honestly don't know if it worked by doing it once. I know after ten times if this is something I want to incorporate into my business or my life. It's not until we reach immersion than we can really tell.

I came back from these conferences with three big goals to tackle in the new year. I'm passionate about doing them. And I know I'll probably begin and then say, this isn't working, or this isn't what I thought, and want to quit.

But I won't. I won't until I do it for sixty days nonstop. Until I know enough to make an informed decision.

What types of things in your life do you want to immerse yourself in? What have you stepped away from you'd like to go back to and try again?

Chapter Forty-One

How to do All the Things and Succeed as a Writer.

Who doesn't want to know the secret of success and how to handle the ever-changing, ever-expanding number of tasks it takes to be or stay relevant in this industry?

Lucky for you, I have all the answers in this post!

It's quite messy out in publishing land lately. I've been in this business for over a decade—even longer—and I believe there is so many good changes. We have more power as writers than we ever had. We have more choices than we ever had.

Unfortunately, this can sometimes lead to chaos. Think of how it was when we had Blockbuster. We had this giant store to pick out DVD's and it was an exciting Friday night, choosing what you felt like watching for the weekend.

Now? I have Netflix, Hulu, Disney, Prime, Peacock and Max. Probably, I have others that I've forgotten to cancel after my free trial. There are literally nights when I want to indulge with a movie and I spend one hour scrolling through endless choices, considering, discarding, until I look at the clock and decide it's now too late to watch a movie so I grab a book instead.

Same thing with books. Endless choices and opportunities at a click. Authors are savvy though, so we've learned everything in order to compete.

There's Facebook and Amazon ads to boost exposure. There's giveaways and list builders. There are influencers and social media. There are subscriptions like Substack and Ream and Patreon. There's Kickstarter for special editions and new projects. There's Shopify and direct sales. There are podcasts. There's blogging. There's YouTube and videos. There are courses galore and we can learn anything we want, whenever we want.

The world is our oyster, forgive the cliché.

So…why are authors burning out by the bucketload? Why are we more miserable and stressed out than ever? Why, when we have endless directions to go?

Because there's too many things to choose from. Many have FOMO. Many have lost our instinct— that guiding light that drives us and speaks to us in the middle of the night – some call it our Muse. It says:

Write this. Do this. Choose this.

Why don't we just listen and stay on our own individual path?

Because we've lost our confidence. The world is too big for us and inside? We're all nerdy, shy, reclusive hermit creatives who are more comfortable with imaginary people. But we're supposed to go out there and pitch and be on camera and sell and interact. We need to go to conferences and be on podcasts and do signings.

The real problem is, my lovelies, we want to do it ALL because then it will finally guarantee success – won't it?

Yeah, I think it will. Because let's be honest. If we were able to run successful ads, meet our readers, network at conferences, be funny and relevant on social media, write fabulous books, make sure they hit all the tropes or are fresh and new as our publishers want, plus put out some special editions with beautiful covers, sell direct and in all the stores plus a few KU's and throw in a serial for Vella and Radish – we are DEFINITELY GOING TO BE SUCCESSFUL.

Because we've covered all our bases.

But, alas, we are not superhuman. We want lives. We are a bunch of whiney babies that say – but what about my family, or spiritual side, or vacations or kids, or keeping house? What about everything else outside of my career?

Yeah – you better give that up if you want guaranteed success.

Have I made everyone angry yet? Did I break the promise of my post?

No. I told you the secret. Do everything and you will be successful.

Oh – you can't? Well, now that's another post. Let's pivot.

I followed the secondary road. I realized I'd like to do it all, because I am a workaholic achiever. But the other parts of me don't mesh well. I have high intellection and relator and empathy and that damn maximizer/developer/input crap. I like to think and ponder. I like to learn things and take my time. I like to do my very best to keep myself connected and happy to my friends and family.

Oh, and I like to do it with a smile – that damn positivity.

I began to learn my lessons this year, and finally after all this time of searching I discovered the answer to success without having to sacrifice the rest of it.

I choose to do some things. I choose to start without waiting for perfection.

Writing comes first. Quality comes first. That's the foundation that everything else hinges on, so if you are a writer reading this with only one book or behind on the writing and a servant to the almighty admin?

Stop and go write more. Just…write. More content equals more possibilities of success.

Okay, you're writing and you have plenty of content. Now you need to pick two things. Just two.

Only two.

Write them down. What do you want most? Dial in to what doesn't make you sick to your stomach but does make you nervous. You need growth which is painful. But you shouldn't be throwing up with nerves. We are looking for that delicious butterfly nervousness in your stomach when you have a first date. It looks tempting. You think you can have it, but you're not sure.

Is it running ads and learning everything you can?

Now write down the second thing. I know choosing two is the hardest part of this exercise. You need to commit though or you will spend the next year spinning out. Believe me, I know. I did this. I lived it. Trust me.

You have two things. Now, you are going to make a plan. You are going to learn everything about it if you are a learner, or you are going to just push through and leap if you're that type of personality and learn along the way.

It doesn't matter how you go about doing these two things. There's not even a timeline on it. You just need to be moving toward the goalpost of launching those two things.

Kickstarter? Learn, then launch.

Ads? Learn, then create ads and launch.

Shopify? Learn, or hire, then launch.

Social Media Success? Learn what videos work, train the algorithm, then launch. Or launch and learn by what's working and what's not.

Subscription? Figure out what levels you want, what you want to offer, and launch.

The key to all of this is to launch. Because you'll figure it out. But if you don't try something, too much time will go by doing nothing except thinking and worrying and planning and feeling frustration.

What if it tanks spectacularly? What if you're humiliated that your Kickstarter didn't fund while every author you know did? What if you have no members showing up at your subscription you spent months working on? What if no one comes to your table at the signing and you're left with a bunch of books to take home in humiliation?

Good for you!

It means you are successful! Because you are doing new things. This means, you are lowering your odds to hit huge heights. And you're learning! You get to tweak and do better next time!

Isn't that fantastic news?

One of the most important things in life we forget about is growth. If we're not growing, we are dying.

You are a leader, not a follower. You lead by your own heart, choosing two things out of hundreds of actions, and you got to learn it, and try it, and figure out if you liked it or if it can really help you in your career like you believed.

Here's the real secret. Lean in.

Just because someone dies by the sword and says Facebook Ads is the best way to gain success, doesn't mean it's true for you.

Same goes for every single item on the list. You don't know what works for you. But you can try and find out.

But you need to start with two things, because this is how you figure out if it's right for you. Now, the second sucky thing about this trying out stuff is it may take time to work. It's not an overnight job.

If you want to invest in a serial story, it may take over a hundred chapters before you can really figure out if it can be a success. It's an investment in time.

But what if you begin writing it, and no one reads it, and months go by and you're not making any money like you've been promised? But you kind of like doing it. And you think about stopping to save time and effort but writing it doesn't suck, and then you can always publish it as a book later so it's not lost content, and you keep going. For you. Because you're learning and doing something new.

What if an entire year goes by and suddenly—you're breaking the top of the charts, and your monthly income starts to increase?

What if it's not the type of money you dreamed of or was promised by others? But what if it's still solid money, and now you have two books you can create out of all those chapter. And now you find you really like this type of writing, so you start another serial story and then it grows faster than the first one and suddenly—you have a whole new segment of success.

Wouldn't that be awesome?

And if it tanks after a year and you feel kind of sucky about it —so what? When you start college, you're immediately forced to take a bunch of pre requisites. You're paying to learn crap like astronomy or medieval history or how to write a persuasive essay. It's irritating. Feels like a waste of time.

But secretly? It's pretty damn cool to know about the stars and the cosmos. Or be able to write a kick ass letter to someone to get an extra discount because they pissed you off. Or find out some weird story about a past knight that makes its way into your brain and allows you to think in a different way.

Was that really a waste? Is learning anything new ever a waste?

No.

And neither is failing.

Pick two things. Learn. Fail. Repeat. And feel damn proud of yourself for not playing things safe. For being a leader in your career and stepping up. For stepping out. For trying.

Aren't we lucky to be writers?

Chapter Forty-Two

Information Overload and Ways to Handle It

I JUST GOT BACK from a full summer of traveling. I literally lived out of a suitcase—it was wonderful and wild and exciting. I'm not complaining about one second of the privilege.

I knew there'd be a price when I got back and I was willing to pay. I took twenty-four hours to get over jet lag and unbury myself from laundry. When I took a breath and became brave enough to open my computer (I'd kept up with email and my ongoing Kickstarter on my laptop but left all the rest) I was overcome by a sense of overwhelm from information overload.

As I sorted through endless back stuff from podcasts I liked, blogs I followed, Substack memberships I paid for, Patreon subscriptions I paid for, self-help mentors, new classes that dropped, and dozens of other things, I began to form a new realization.

Sometimes, helpful information and learning can be too much.

Especially in this new age. I love seeing all the new subscriptions popping up (Hello, I did one with Ream!). There are multiple community groups that are dynamic and full of helpful information. I'm thrilled at the advice and tips dropping daily in my inbox which will help me bump my sales on platforms, tweak my Amazon algorithms, make more money in my direct store, write better, market better, sell better, etc.

I bought another Facebook ads course. I bought a course that will help me streamline my Shopify store. I bought a workshop on the Enneagram to give me key insights into my writing personality. I bought a ProWriting editor program to help me write faster and better. I bought a course for self-help with Tony Robbins because I love the way he makes me feel clear and empowered. I have online workshops to watch from InkersCon.

And it keeps coming. Once I click on something interesting, I'm immediately recommended to other sites I may like, and even though I don't remember if I signed up, I begin to receive more emails, with tons of amazing things to teach me and show me and help me.

When does it all become too much? When does learning begin to actually impede our progress with our writing and career? How do we make hard decisions to sort through the things that are priority and the things we can drop?

And if you're like me, maybe you're afraid to hit unsubscribe or not buy that hot new course that will push us to a higher income level and more success like we all crave?

It's exhausting. We are lucky, but it's time to make some hard decisions. Like a wild flowering rosebush, our minds need to be carefully pruned and cut back so we can grow again in a better controlled environment. It seems cruel to cut all those healthy branches, doesn't it? But if we don't, the rose eventually dies.

If we keep going, our brains may explode from too many possibilities and ideas and promises.

This realization has been nagging at the back of my brain for a while, but returning to work after an extended break will also give a brutal sense of clarity. It allows us to get out of the mess and take a hard look at what we really need, and what we really don't.

Yes, reading posts and learning and trying to be better is important. But in our unending quest, we can become numb. We become an addictive scroller. Our attention begins to wane because we are looking at too much so we learn nothing.

There is nothing I love more than a lazy Sunday morning catching up on reading the things I love. There are delicious Substack posts and daily digests. There are the new podcasts that drop and YouTube videos of my favorite people sharing treasure chests of advice or insights. There are new classes I want to watch.

There's always a great online sale for shoes or purses.

Too many times, I look up and hours have passed. My brain should be excited and ready to input all of these wonderful things, but instead?

I feel completely overwhelmed. I feel like there's so much I'm behind on, how can one tiny thing help me? I need to write more books and do more tasks to get ahead. In a matter of minutes, all that helpful information I ingested can turn into a bite of depression and the desire to hide from all of it.

It feels so much easier to just let it all go rather than doing one thing. Our poor brains can't multitask. That's just a word we use to get jobs on interviews. Sure, I can do a bunch of things if I need to, but it's not the true normal state of our brains.

Now that I alarmed everyone, how on earth do we try and scale back to what we really need?

I don't know.

Well, I know what I need to do. But since we are all unique, and thrive with various subjects and pressure levels, I can only offer advice to help you stare down your own inbox and make hard decisions.

First, I began with how my gut and body feels after I read something. Am I excited? Am I soothed? Do I feel like I can take a deep breath from my stomach and see a vision of me doing what that person or group advised me to do?

Sometimes, it's a hard no. I have subscriptions with people inspire me to do better, but after listening to the podcast, reading their book, or taking their class, I mostly feel like a failure. I want to do it. I want to be like them.

But I never will.

I unsubscribe.

There are also places I go to rest and relax. Entertainment and fun lists of favorite things. I pick my favorites to keep because all work and no play will make us all implode.

Many of my subscriptions I find myself skipping over because I don't feel a burning need to read it, or I'm not excited to see the updates. Maybe there was something in the past I liked and got on a mailing list. I unsubscribe to all of those, even though there's random posts I like.

I treat the above like cleaning my closets.

Will I wear this? Maybe.

Do I like it? Kind of.

Do I need to lose ten pounds in order to wear it? Yes.

Can I imagine myself wearing it by next week? No.

Donate.

I love courses, too. All the courses. But I'm beginning to see I've overindulged. I've set a weekly schedule now to carve out an hour or two throughout the five day work week where I just rest and listen to a course with my notepad on my lap. Or I get on the treadmill for an hour and instead of watching the newest installment of Love is Blind, I listen to a podcast. My ambition and thirst for success are a gift, but it's time for a good pruning so I don't burn out.

Social media is next. That's an entire other place where we get our info, from TikTok recipes, book reviewers, friend updates, dog/cat videos, new releases, and shopping. Not much to unsubscribe to here, but I've paired down my sites to only three I regularly check. Three is enough.

It's time to re-direct all this wonderful information and help in a way we can truly thrive and not become overwhelmed.

A great place to start is your inbox. What are you receiving regularly? What do you automatically delete and not think about? What do you get excited to read immediately? What hits you with a lukewarm feeling? What emails feel like clothing you'll wear after you get to that magical weight?

Be honest. Many can also be from friends, which is supportive, but if you have fifty author newsletters and your inbox is draining your time and energy, it's time for an unsubscribe.

Take some time and do your own intake analysis. Be brutally honest.

Keep what excites you or aligns with who you are now. You may have some old subscriptions you've simply outgrown. A good pruning is a perfect task to do when you reach a new quarter or season.

Chapter Forty-Three

What Happened When I Re-Married my Husband

I THINK my title was a bit misleading but not really. Let me explain.

My husband and I hit our 20th anniversary this summer and celebrated by renewing our vows in Nashville, at a little chapel with our closest friends and family. The officiant was Elvis.

It was epic.

Most of us weren't sure how it would be—many of my friends thought it would be a fun, cheesy good time that didn't mean much. But the ceremony ended up being more profound than our first wedding. It was completely different and very much needed.

My first wedding? I was pregnant with my son (it wasn't technically a shotgun wedding since we'd already been engaged – he was just a bit of an early surprise!)

Though I was in my mid-thirties, we were still a bit wild. We partied hard on weekends, traveled, and basically lived a free type of life where we did what we wanted, when we wanted. Then, suddenly, I was pregnant, planning a wedding, and looking for a house. It was a stressful time for us, and though the wedding was beautiful, it was completely dissatisfying for me, personally.

My husband hung out with his friends all night and ignored me. I was carrying extra weight, hormonal, and not in the best frame of mind. Needless to say, the next morning I gave him crap and that day has always been a bit overshadowed by my poor memories. When people rave about how great my wedding was, I grunt and glare at my husband. He's apologized multiple times but I told him clearly that there was only one way to make it up to me.

A complete re-do on our twentieth anniversary.

He said yes, of course. I mean, no one thought we'd actually get to twenty years, not because we didn't think our marriage would last but we didn't think we'd ever get that old!

This upcoming year, he was stunned when I reminded him of his promise and promptly told him what I wanted.

An Elvis wedding. In Nashville—my absolute favorite place to party. I wanted the ceremony to be completely different. I wanted to own my re-do on my terms. He agreed.

We flew out with thirteen people for the weekend. I wore a short lace dress and cowboy boots. I felt prettier than I did twenty years ago, even though I was heavier than in my pregnancy and much older.

Because inside my skin, I was so much more of a badass. I knew who I was. I was a mom. I'd gone through numerous struggles with myself and my marriage and fought my way through. My husband was not romantic. In fact, he's known as one of the most unromantic men ever—which make people laugh when they found out I write romance for a living.

Yet, that day, in front of Elvis, he poured out his heart in his own vows and stunned everyone in the chapel. We cried together. Recommitted to this life together, which now we knew didn't guarantee passion and promise and only good times. But God, it meant so much more than first time.

When we danced to Elvis, I felt like the moment was just for us, and not for the guests staring on, or a photographer snapping endless pictures.

We had a big dinner then partied endlessly on the rooftops till 3am. We danced, sang in the streets, and ate quesadillas from food trucks, drunk on alcohol and joy.

And when we returned home, things had just leveled up. We were more careful with each other. Paid more attention. We'd reminded ourselves we chose each other; separate from the minutia that made up our days and nights. It was freeing and romantic in its own quiet way.

Why am I sharing all this personal stuff?

Because my new wedding reminded me that it's the same with all the things in our lives, especially writing.

It's so easy to stay on the treadmill, cranking out new books; marketing with social media videos; editing and sharing and updating nonstop, always stuck in the daily details.

But I'm different now. I'm not chasing fame to see who I am. I'm not chasing approval from readers or editors (well, maybe sometimes?) as I write for the masses. With fifty books behind me, I've leveled up.

I've had bad books and good books. I've had terrible rejections and disappointments, and amazing opportunities. I've been poor and I've been rich and I've been in between. This relationship I have with writing is important.

Sometimes, it needs a pause. A re-do. A re-commitment.

We are not the same writers as when we start. Each book changes us—gets us closer to figuring out who we are and how we see the world. What our real stories are. What we want to explore now.

So, I did a vow renewal as a writer.

I promised to write through good and bad.

I promised to honor the process and my Muse, even when it's difficult and makes me frustrated and pissy.

I promised to have faith that no matter how things change, it will all be okay.

Write Free

I promised to remember to enjoy the work more during the journey, and not its results on social media or from others reactions.

I promised to never give up, and learn how to pivot if needed. Flexibility is needed in any type of relationships.

The other day, I opened up my fifty sixth manuscript. I wrote a scene while listening to Taylor Swift's The Tortured Poet's Department. My dogs snoozed on their pillows beside me. The day was gloomy as I stared outside, waiting for my Muse to come up with the next answer for the rest of the scene. A hot cup of coffee sat on my mug warmer beside me. My desk was filled with pieces of papers, lists, books, stuffed animals, and items that made me happy. As I thought over my characters and how their beginning would eventually reach the end. I reminded myself that even though I was only at 5K and had thousands of words left to write, it would all happen if I took it day by day; hour by hour; word by word. A feeling of incredible joy and peace came over me.

And I smiled.

Do you have anything in your life you'd like to re-commit to?

Chapter Forty-Four

What Makes me Happy

I was listening to a YouTube video of Sarra Cannon. She's the creator of a fabulous planning strategy called HB90, which was extremely helpful to me for trying to implement my overwhelming work life into bite size, goal-oriented pieces.

Sarra has a passion for planners and notebooks. In this particular video, she took viewers through a pile of her newest planners and notebooks, showing us how she tweaked each one to specifically fit her style and mood. She dazzled us with her vast array of stickers, markers, inserts, and covers, taking us on a journey I'd never think could be so inspiring.

I was mesmerized. I watched the hour presentation and afterward, I went immediately to all the sites she recommended to shop. Suddenly, I had a thirst to create my very own unique planner and fill up various notebooks.

After my shopping hangover, I began to think over why something I'd normally not be into struck me so wholeheartedly, driving me to buy and experience all the things she did in her video.

And the answer struck.

Joy.

Sarra was brimming with joy as she took us through her process. We didn't even see her face! It was just her hands and voice in the video as she pulled items out in front of the camera. But each word she spoke vibrated with true delight and the excitement she was feeling to show us all the things that made her happy.

I got swept up her in positive and simple contentment of doing and sharing what she loved.

The realization inspired me. I began to think about the things that made me smile and feel giddy, but most were steeped around expectations. Sometimes, when I share things on my platform, I get too caught up in the presentation and the logistics, forgetting to focus on my simple love for what I'm sharing.

I began to think back to my younger days where things were simpler, and there were no expectations about anything except happiness.

I immediately grabbed my pen and made a list. I kept my head out of it and followed my gut.

This is what I wrote down:

- The Scholastic Book Fair
- Going to the library
- Going to the bookstore
- Going to see a movie in the theater
- The feel and smell of a new book
- A brand-new notebook to write my thoughts in
- Music
- A carnival with rides and treats in the parking lot of our mall
- Rolling down a hill in the freshly cut lawn
- Climbing trees and hanging on a thick branch while I daydreamed
- Beautiful fresh pens and white crisp paper

and a new box of the Crayola crayons with the sharpener in the back
- Long car rides staring out the window
- Petting dogs and horseback riding

That's it. When I began thinking too hard, I put down my pen. It was enough.

When I go over this list it's mostly things from when I was fifteen years old and younger. As I grew, the pleasures changed because life got more complicated. But each time I read one of those items on my list, I sighed in pleasure.

I remember how books smelled and the sound of the pages being flipped, standing in the aisle of the bookstore while I carefully perused my choices. I knew my parents only had the money for one book. Not two. What would I choose? How could such a decision invoke such delicious dread and joy at the same time?

When I read my list, I also realize nothing really has changed. Most of the things I still love and treasure. I just don't pause to enjoy them with the same zeal I had before.

I may not roll down a hill or climb trees, but after my lawn is mowed, I'm drawn to wander outside and suck in massive deep breaths. I become dizzy at the fresh clean scent.

Every time I see a good tree with thick twisted branches, I comment to my husband that it would be a wonderful tree to climb. My fingers tingle with anticipation but my mind quickly shuts the thought down. Before, I saw possibilities at that height. Now, I see possibilities of a broken bone, lol.

I'm still obsessed with pens and papers. I look at a box of Crayola with greed, and can recite all the colors that make each crayon sound extra special.

When I sit with my boys at a movie theater, bathed in darkness, fingers stuck in the bucket of salty, buttery popcorn, previews flickering across the giant screen, I still experience a shiver of excitement.

These joys are ingrained in my memory. They are part of my soul.

I don't want to forget them anymore. Because steeping myself in the memories reminds me to bring my current experiences to life. It can be fleeting but we need to grab onto more joyous smiling moments on this journey, even as we are intensely focused towards more important things.

But what if the most important thing in the world are those precious seconds of smiling as you gaze up at a mighty gnarled oak tree, imagining yourself perched on that perfect branch, hidden from the world yet feeling powerful?

The Scholastic book fair was an event that I spent days thinking about; planning for; dreaming of. I remember every small detail, from the racks of books lined up in the cafeteria, scratching my pencil across the checkboxes for each book, to the long dialogue with my parents as I begged and begged for more…citing education while my heart beat wildly, waiting for their answer.

I feel the same way today. I'm excited each time I buy a book but have I acknowledged how powerful it feels to get to choose? No one is going to tell me no or limit my inventory. I should feel drunk on my power.

I need to tap into that memory and connect with it more deeply. After all, I dreamed of this moment over and over as a child. The feeling of buying tons of books on my own. Of reading as many as I wanted on my terms. Of being able to stay up as late as I want, reading those same books.

I want to re-discover my passion for things that bring me joy.

I never want to take buying a book for granted. Or the trees. Or the feel of a blank new page and a smooth Sharpie ready to create…anything.

What is on your joy list? Write one for yourself and see how it makes you feel!

Chapter Forty-Five

How to Create Emotional Sex Scenes

Let's talk about sex.

As writers of romance, we know sex is integral in our books, and that doesn't necessarily mean the whole open-door-dirty-talking scenes. It can be as simple as a kiss. A touch.

Hell, I once read a book crackling with so much sexual tension, it ended with a kiss at the last chapter and had me hooked.

So, how do we get our readers to be completely invested in the hero and heroine's connection—even we're not comfortable or don't like writing steam on the page?

Let's dig in and find ways to make it happen.

Sexual tension: I believe this is the key to keeping things moving forward. The buildup of banter, and uncomfortable feelings each feel toward the other is a great way to keep readers engaged. If you're using dialogue to build those types of scenes, don't forget to use your other senses to enhance the interaction. Incorporate action tags and physical reactions.

Example:

"You think you know how do everything, boss man?" she challenged.

He stared at her. "Yes. If you were doing your job the way I expect, you'd know, too."

Anger poured through her veins. She was going to kill him. "And if you took a moment to listen to anyone other than yourself, you'd realize this deal is a mistake."

A frown creased his brow. "I listened to the team and made the right decision."

She tossed her hair. "I'll prove it to you."

"Fine, it's a bet. Just make sure when I win, you remember I never lose."

I know this example is rough, lol, but let's take it and transform so we can add that crackle needed in a good romance.

"You think you know how do everything, boss man?" she challenged.

That full lower lip quirked, but his face remained cool and expressionless. She tried to ignore the unique scent of clove and spice rising from his skin. Awareness swirled in the air with his scent and made Claire question her plan to confront him. Her stomach was already dancing with nerves and he seemed to be unmoved by her words. "Yes. If you were doing your job the way I expect, you'd know, too."

He'd already dismissed her, with his clipped voice and icy gray eyes and masculine body. Lean muscles filled out the starched dress shirt, pulling tight across his chest. She imagined her fingers smoothing over the soft material, sinking her nails into the hard strength beneath the civility. Anger poured through her veins. She was going to kill him. "And if you took a moment to listen to anyone other than yourself, you'd realize this deal is a mistake."

Claire uttered the words with a fierce plea she'd desperately tried to hide. Not that he'd care. She meant nothing to him but a lowly assistant. Preparing herself for him to stalk away, she tried not to look fazed when a frown creased his brow. He took a step forward and closed the distance. The air crackled with tension and something more…something she didn't want to probe. "I listened to the team and made the right decision."

His gaze fused with hers. Implacable authority steamed from his pores, making her a bit weak; a bit needy. Why did his awful, arrogant behavior ignite both her temper and a need to strip away his surface to find what he was hiding? Secrets blazed in those gray eyes. Claire ached to be the woman he revealed them to.

Instead, she fought her weakness and tossed her hair. "I'll prove it to you."

Claire expected her biting retort to either be ignored or dismissed with a casual flick of his hand. Instead, one brow rose and he leaned forward, face inches from hers. She studied the curve of his lip; carved cheekbones; sloping jaw. His voice dipped and stroked her belly, his words shattering all those safe words she'd built in order to function around him. "Fine, it's a bet. Just make sure when I win, you remember I never lose."

Again – the example is rough but see what a difference filling in all those other senses brings to the scene? Tension is about scent, and voice. Of where they stand next to each other and their inner thoughts. Imagining a kiss or a touch or the feel of skin underneath clothes. Close your eyes and go remember textures, scents, sounds, and tastes.

Create an emotional wound to heal: Characters need a growth arc and conflict to conquer. This should pertain to both the hero and heroine. An emotional wound is a great way to bring the characters close together and allow softening. Connecting to the very human fragility of our inner doubts and challenges is something we all share. Is there anything better than a growly alpha male who's suddenly understood by the heroine? Like the beast with a thorn in his paw and once it's removed, he views the one who helped him in a different light. Same with the heroine—by finally glimpsing vulnerabilities of the hero, hearts soften. These wound scenes are critical to change the pacing and heighten the intimacy.

Think of the simple animated movie, Beauty and the Beast. The beast is hurt by the wolves saving Belle, but when they get back to the castle, she tends to his wounds. Pressing a medicated rag to the blood, he spits and groans in pain, but then calms as she cleans the wounds with a caring touch. The beast is hungry for such affection, and the care from her is suddenly full of words unspoken. Belle recognizes his sacrifice to save her, and that he has vulnerabilities hidden beneath the surface. Things change in that scene between them. It's a turning point. Use these types of connection to build the physical intimacy. It can be a kiss; a touch; or a seething look. It all works if underneath is emotion that is pulling us forward.

Write free with no restrictions: What is the biggest sexual organ? The brain. When we write, if we're worried about being embarrassed, or sounding stupid, we will never really be able to immerse ourselves into sexual scenes. It's critical we write brave and free. If you're getting tripped up with these mental blocks, try free writing for three full pages nonstop, getting all your doubts and fears on the page, then try to write the scene again.

We need to remember any type of physical interaction is part of love and being human. There is no shame in writing physical connection in any way you choose. If it comes out awkward and you feel silly, who cares? Push through the scene and then go back and see if there are any lines you liked, or feelings it evoked. Those are the ones you keep. It's mining for gold. We cannot be good at everything we write, so we practice our limitations.

Write scenes that make your heart beat and excite you.

Sometimes, I'm excited about getting to a particular scene I know will be fun to write, or offer a challenge. Maybe it's a pivot for the hero and heroine, or the chance to bring them together for an intimate moment. If a scene is giving you pleasure, lean into it and try to build more connection between them. Pull apart the scene and experiment with what may make it stronger.

For example, have one of them comfort the other. Or care for the other when sick. Or see past a barrier to their true soul. Let a character finally feel seen. Expose vulnerability or a secret from their past.

This is the best time to structure a kiss, or embrace or a sex scene. Instead of getting technical about what body part goes where, or what clothes come off and how, let yourself carried away with the experience of being open and vulnerable to another. It's such a powerful moment in romance. You can always go back and take care of the technical parts. I can't tell you how many times I'm swept away with the scene but later, have to edit to explain how they got to the kitchen to the bedroom, or how his shirt is suddenly off, or how his hand can be in her hair when it's cupping her breast. That's fixable and not important. The emotion is what brings the scene forward.

Some various tips to up the sexy in your scenes:

Dirty talk or Naughty talk. Or a special

endearment one calls the other. Even a mocking phrase can become intimate later on.

A surprise erotic gesture, like a bite to the lower lip, teeth sinking into a neck or shoulder, a gentle squeeze and lingering caress.

Use the eyes. Gazes locking together to unveil emotions makes a reader sigh with pleasure.

Description. Don't forget to tell us what your hero and hero are wearing. What they smell like. How their voices sound. If their skin is rough or soft. Use colors. Use strong verbs.

Experiment with this: write a kiss scene that takes up half a page. Just a kiss. The set up, the kiss and the afterward. Draw it out and linger. Then go back to see what your favorite parts are.

Use other authors and books. I love to mark phrases or scenes that make my heart beat fast – scribble it down in notes and take it apart to find out why you love it so much. It's important because it means you think it's sexy.

Use banter/dialogue – flirting is always in style. Keep your hero and heroine aware of each other even in action or suspense is happening. Even arguing is a connection.

Listen to music while you write to get out of your head.

If you write sweet, challenge yourself to write spicy. If you write spicy, challenge yourself to write a sweeter scene that has sexual tension.

Go forth, my peeps, and write a love scene!

Chapter Forty-Six

How Disney Reminds me of Living in the Moment

I just got back from Disney on a family vacation.

I'm very lucky I'm able to take my family. When I was growing up, I went nowhere. We had no money and our big trip was a weekend at Hershey Park, which we talked about weeks before and afterward. It didn't matter because summer vacation was wonderful no matter what we got to do.

Most of the time, it was my brother and I running wild in the neighborhood, sitting in apple trees and stealing the fruit; exploring the wood and running from the cows and bulls that grazed in a nearby farm; playing Kick the Can in the streets after dinner while mosquitoes feasted and fireflies lit up the dark. Summer is everything in my mind.

But now I'm blessed to take my boys to Disney and we all love it. They are nineteen and seventeen and still love riding all the childhood rides along with the big ones. They enjoy the classics and the occasional character meeting. They love the food and snacks and parades and fireworks. They are joyous in that rare way when our days revolve around our next meal or the next activity. Walking almost ten miles per day in the scorching heat was part of the joy, even as sweat clung to our clothes and we guzzled water by the gallon so we wouldn't faint.

I watched them in line playing Head's Up and the question game, where we have twenty questions to guess the Disney character. Phones were tucked away.

Even at dinner, there was no outside world sneaking in. No emails or work for my husband and I. No deadlines or pressures or even the political shitstorm. No Facebook or IG or TikTok. I took pictures but didn't post. I was greedy of my time, so precious and fleeting as my boys grow and change and take steps further away.

Disney is magic for those reasons. We felt as if we dropped through a portal and able to cherish every second, whether we were drenched in sweat, missed the bus, waited in overlong lines, or walked with blisters. We were truly present.

When this happens to me, I am now able to not only recognize the moments but savor them. I wasn't able to do that when I was younger. I raced from one great moment to the next and chased the high. I hated the lows. Now, they are one; twisted into a great rope and braided so tightly I cannot distinguish one from the other. Maybe it's age. Maybe it's the time of year because summer is always my high time. Maybe it's realizing I'm grateful for what I have, because I can see clearly the people I have lost, or the experiences that bring grief and pain.

In Disney, it's just the now. I know we cannot live in vacation, but it was hard morphing back to regular life. I love my office, I love my work, I love my dogs and my house and my surroundings. Yet, I'm still misty with longing to truly saturate myself in the day to day, and live moment to moment.

Disney is my reminder to stop and breathe and ponder. To wait in line with only my thoughts and the heat and the sound of my boys laughing. To eat new food and see new things. To watch my surroundings so I don't miss anything.

To pay attention. To be.

When we got home, I'd missed an important deadline. My oldest got sick. One of the cars wouldn't start. The dog had thrown up on the nice rug and the stain wouldn't come out. Silly, annoying things we deal with daily.

I thought of Disney with a longing sigh, then turned my attention on what I had. Today. All parts of it.

During dinner, we chatted about our vacation; my son's summer college class; their plans for the rest of the week. We played Unstable Unicorns. My son took a nap and felt better. We caught up on tv shows and ate ice pops and sat with the dogs in our lap.

We enjoyed being home.

With a Disney mindset.

Does vacation remind you of those moments, too?

Chapter Forty-Seven

The Power of Reinvention

I admit it.

I'm a Swiftie.

It started slow, but I eventually became infatuated with not only her music, but her business savvy. At how a young, popular, single female was able to break through so many societal constraints and use her voice. To advocate for herself and her fans. To say it was okay to want to make a lot of money. Her authenticity spoke to me.

And if you don't like Taylor Swift? That's okay. I'm more interested in breaking down the choices in her career and how she taught me and the world about the power of reinvention. That you can retreat from the world and shut it all down, then emerge triumphant.

Or for others? Maybe just re-emerge with the hope of future success. It depends on how you judge success.

Some say making a million dollars. Or writing fifty books. Or making a bestseller list.

Others say to have family safe and healthy around them. A place to live. Or being able to get out of bed in the morning and face the day.

All are valid. What I like about Swift is she's been at multiple levels, too. An unknown trying to make it in the music world. A young musician learning her craft and navigating fame. Morphing her personal life into her music. Dealing with social media and deciding what type of relationship she wanted with her fans. Growing up and making mistakes as the world watched and judged. Breaking down and retreating in total burnout. Dealing with shame and anger and demons. Then stepping back out, in her revenge dress, with two new albums and no longer afraid of being who she is.

Don't we all go through this? Whether it's career or personal life, we are always facing challenges and have choices how to move forward. Sometimes, retreat is best for healing. And then I know there are times when I've hidden for too long, and though it makes me nauseous, it's time to step out of my safe place and take risks again.

We get to reinvent ourselves over and over. Every morning, we step out of bed and grab a brand-new chance. We don't have to carry the past or our mistakes with us. We can put on our revenge dress and fling the door open. We can stay in our comfy pjs and watch tv in bed.

But we get to choose.

Watching Taylor Swift reminds me of my own power.

My hope?

That we all step into ours, no matter what our decisions are.

Chapter Forty-Eight

Relevancy and Becoming a Mentor

(Originally posted on Women Writers, Women(s) Books)

I'VE BEEN THINKING a lot lately about the new writers flooding the marketplace successfully. It's very exciting to watch so much talent find their niche and blossom. Whether it's via TikTok or ads, KU opportunities or breaking out in a hot genre, for me it's a reminder of hope and how this career can consistently reward patience and perseverance.

And sometimes, not.

It's difficult when you write a great book, confident with all of the content and tropes and audience, sure the cover is spot on and every other factor is pointed toward breakout or success. When it doesn't happen, the frustration and confusion can really play a game with our brains. The voices begin, questioning and doubting your validity, your story, and your right to be in this marketplace.

For a writer with a solid number of books in the background and a previous break-out, it can be a reminder we are no longer in the spotlight. We had our time to feel the sun bright on our face; to watch book clubs or readers fuss over the book, to feel confident as we attend writer's conferences and be sought after for advice or mentorship, even being asked to do keynotes.

Success is a heady feeling. It's addictive. And when you are sometimes only as good as your last book, writing as a full-time career is not for the faint of heart.

At the core, stripped of all the frills of an audience and outside validation, there must be some sort of true love for the work. For me, my entire life has been about writing. It is the way I process my life and the world around me. I think in terms of story. I want to die with my laptop or a book in my lap, still chasing the end.

But as a seasoned veteran still fighting my way for continued success in a world that has changed so drastically, I sometimes wonder if that is simply the way of life. The student of writing becomes the seasoned veteran and then the teacher/mentor. Some like this shift; others fight it, afraid the work will disappear into good intentions and other tasks in search of feeling that hit of adrenalin again.

I was thinking about the movie *The Color of Money*. It's the sequel to the famous movie, *The Hustler*, starring Paul Newman. Newman is the brash, overconfident student, hot to take on the veteran in the world of pool. Newman believes if he can beat him, he will finally occupy the top slot in pool—be the top dog. He wants that crown more than anything.

In *The Color of Money*, Newman has grown up and moved past chasing the competition. He's happily slipped into the role of mentor, teaching his students how to hustle pool and win money. When Tom Cruise shows up, Newman realizes he's a diamond in the rough—he's got crazy talent and can win. Being young and cocky, Cruise emits some behavior Newman did in his past, and the audience is treated to the continuous circle of life, watching it play out.

Who is young becomes old. What is new becomes learned. Plus, the external environment around Newman changes drastically. He gets excited to bring Cruise to an old bar well known for pool, but when they get there, it's been closed down. Cruise laughs and mocks his teacher, but the expression on Newman's face is familiar and heartbreaking.

Why did this change? Why did it have to change? This is what I know!

But it does change. Cruise has the advantage there, and knows it. He wants to go out on his own and prove it.

The part of the movie that fascinated me the most was when Newman realized he wanted to play pool, too. Not for a hustle. Not to teach Cruise. He wanted to play pool because he loved it with his heart and soul, and he wasn't done. He decided to challenge himself as both a master and student all over again, refusing to surrender who he was to every up-and-coming talent around him.

Was it wrong? Should Newman have stepped politely aside and left the game to the younger generation? Was his time up and he stayed too long?

Or was it his right as an expert in that world, to decide on his own? Professionals go in and out of retirement all the time. Sometimes, the voice inside is screaming: I'm not done yet! I still have so many things to show the world!

For me, I think it's a wonderful thing to keep pushing forward. I believe if there is still a burning desire, that's good enough to step back into the competition without needing to make any explanations.

At the same time, we need to recognize many of our roles will be taken away and given to the newcomers. I also believe we have a responsibility to mentor and offer what we can to the ones behind us, with grace and kindness.

When *The Marriage Bargain* broke out, I was thrown into a different world. I'd written for thirty years with no money, and suddenly my book was on the NY Times, read in trains, out in Target and I was suddenly well known. The years that followed were on a high but eventually, things calmed down and steadied. There were more gentle ebbs and flows. I surfed the water and took everything the industry gave me: wipeouts, giant waves; and absolute stillness.

Write Free

Looking at some authors who have exploded on the scene, killing it regularly on the Amazon charts or making lists, going viral on social media and featured in bookstores everywhere, I smile and remember. I feel such pride and happiness for the excitement of that part—finally being able to write with a solid audience of readers who anticipate your books is like no other feeling in the world. I hope they're not too stressed or too worried about keeping their spot. I worry they don't burn out under the pressure. I hope they enjoy every moment and it lasts a long, long time.

Then I go back to write my own books. I work on different types of stories now. I'm able to create deeper, more nuanced books after years of practice. I learn TikTok and open up a Shopify store to sell direct. I write a serial story because it's fun and different. I run ads and speak. I do endless admin amidst the writing.

I lean in to the changes instead of bitching. I stay in the game because I'm a writer in my heart and soul, and there is no other way for me. I look to the future, wondering what's next, and take a deep breath instead of cringing. And I try to help anyone who's right behind, exploding their own career and maneuvering around the land mines.

God knows, I stepped on dozens. It would be so nice to warn others where they are hidden.

The writing world is always full of multi-level creatives at various points in their career. I honor each step of the process, and feel grateful for the ones that helped me as I climbed the ladder. Because they are part of my history.

It makes me happy to think I can be a small part of someone else's.

I keep writing and learning to preserve mine.

Everyone is relevant. Everyone gets to choose how they will shape their own path, in career and life.

There's room for both the student and teacher; the ones at the top and the ones at the bottom; and a whole bunch of middles.

Embracing every role with an open mind and heart will provide not only relevance, but in my opinion, some well-needed peace.

Chapter Forty-Nine

Tropes That Get a Bad Rap

Tropes have become hot.

They've always been here, of course. A cornerstone of storytelling everywhere, but many readers didn't know why they loved certain books until we began teasing out this wonderful thing called tropes. Tropes are certain storylines woven into books. They are the building blocks where plot and conflict live. Most of all?

They are about emotion. What readers respond to, and what writers love to explore.

Romance is one of the genres it's known for the most, and it's become so popular, authors now use actual graphics to entice readers to buy based on certain tropes.

Some examples of tropes?

Marriage of convenience/forced proximity – when the hero and heroine strike a bargain to be together, or decide to bargain/marry for convenience. It's a trope I love because forcing the characters together in such an intimate situation is rife for conflict, tension, and eventually, love. See my entire Marriage to a Billionaire series for this one.

Enemies to lovers – one of my faves! The hero and heroine dislike each other in the beginning, and then slowly as the book develops, learn to respect, then love the other. It's a trope perfect for incorporating delicious sexual tension into their banter. Many of my books feature this popular trope, especially *The Start of Something Good* and *Love on Beach Avenue*.

Fake dating – the hero and heroine decide to strike a bargain and pretend they are dating in order to serve a higher purpose. This example is shown in my book, So it Goes, where my hero and heroine pretend to be together to be each other's dates for their family weddings, and try to side step overbearing and nosy relatives. Another is *Book of the Month*, where my heroine saves the hero's bankrupt business so he can break her heart, and she can create another emotional bestseller.

There are a ton more but these give you an idea.

By using tropes, readers can find more of what they love in a book without endlessly scrolling and searching. And for authors?

It's a goldmine of opportunity. By properly using tropes, we're able to craft a stronger story with intention.

If you want a deep dive check out Jennifer Hilt, who's kind of a master teaching and discussing tropes and how they help writers here:

She does some fabulous break-downs and is the author of the Trope Thesaurus, a must-have book for your shelf.

I've also found that in the pursuit of readers finding tropes they love, there's been a lot of blowbacks on the tropes they don't love. Sometimes, specific graphics or posts actually call out the tropes books are avoiding in order to court readers.

After seeing a few of these tropes mentioned multiple times, I thought it would be fun to write a post about the ones that get a bad rap, and the ones I happen to love even though it's not popular opinion!

THE THIRD ACT BREAK-UP:

When I was learning to write a great romance novel, the third act break-up was part of the craft. There's a formula to many romance novels, which too many people translate as lazy or cliché writing.

I disagree.

Formula can be a warm blanket and comfort wrapped around a reader. Knowing there will be a happy ever after in romance novels no matter how much conflict and pain the hero and heroine suffer through, creates an expectation that's important to our reader. Niche genre has a formula. Within the formula, authors put their own fingerprint on a story to make it unique.

The third act break up used to be a staple in romance. This plays out when the hero and heroine reach the black moment, and something happens that breaks them up. With bad writing, a simple misunderstanding can break up the couple, but I'm not talking about that device in this post. Personally, if this is the only conflict breaking up the couple, I won't keep reading.

Write Free

A good third-act breakup will eventually lead to a revelation they are meant to be with one another, and sometimes, a grand gesture. A heartfelt, big apology is one of my favorites. Extra points for a creative grovel.

But as time passed, authors began to break away from that unwritten rule and write love stories without any break-ups. This didn't mean the hero and heroine had no conflict; it simply meant they didn't actually sever the relationship during this difficult time.

I have no issue with this. I love a book without a third act break-up. But lately, reading so many books that clearly avoid it at all costs, and gleefully pointing it out to readers as an advantage, made me sad.

Because I love a good break-up.

I can write an epic break-up.

There's something emotional about the hero or heroine deciding they can't be with each other. Done well, it will lead back to an inner belief within the character, or a hidden fear that surfaces.

When this couple I've been invested in breaks up, I feel as if there's more to lose between them.

Especially when one moves away, dates someone else, or tries to soldier on without their soulmate. It rips me apart. Sign me up for the pain.

I also believe it makes the grand gesture of getting back together a bigger pay off. I'm a sucker for a great break-up and make-up, and some of my favorite romance authors are masters at this plot device. It's makes way for such a great grovel, too. Another one of my ID hits, lol.

Now, I must admit a third act breakup won't do well unless the reasons are real to the reader and the story. But if the author does their job?

I'm in.

CHEATING:

Oh, yeah this is controversial. And I do understand why this could be a trigger and big dislike for readers.

Here's my admission.

I don't mind cheating in my romance books. Of course, it depends on the circumstance and how the author uses the trope.

I want a good reason. I want to feel that the character cheated because they needed to, or had to, or felt as if the cheating allowed them to release the past and put them on a new road.

Maybe I'm a forgiving reader?

I think this trope works best when there's a lot of angst in a book. Younger characters who get into relationships and are confused; where temptation lurks in the shadows. Like lusting after your boyfriend's best friend who's currently in a terrible relationship. The taboo makes the stakes ridiculously high and the conflict is baked in.

I don't need my hero or heroine to have a perfect past. I've forgiven alpha hole heroes who cheated in the past, and I can forgive a heroine with a good enough reason, as long as there's growth or remorse.

I have a cheating a-hole in one of my current books and intend to redeem him. The idea makes me salivate with the challenge.

LOVE TRIANGLE:

I'm not sure if this trope is as hated as the above, but I've seen many book influencers and readers mark this as one of their most disliked. Maybe it goes hand in hand with cheating?

Either way, the idea of a love triangle is a classic – going all the way to one of my fave older series, Beverly Hills 90210 and Dawson's Creek. Should Dylan be with Kelly or Brenda? Should Joey be with Pacey or Dawson?

Hell, when I was reading Archie comics I was obsessed with Veronica and Betty! (I was a huge Veronica fan so I tend to like the bad girl.)

There's a big investment for readers, and big, messy emotions. I love that in my romance. I ended up writing the Red series specifically so I could create an angsty, steamy, soapy reality show of my own making with cliffhangers and cheating and love triangles!

THIRD PERSON POV:

This isn't a trope – it's a narrative technique, but I figured I'd throw in a bonus.

When did this get to be the scorn in the romance world? I learned my entire craft writing third person. Oh, sure, first person POV is nice because of the in-depth perspective in the book. Feeling as if you are the one experiencing the angst and sex and emotion is powerful. Some stories scream for that type of deep dive.

But what about the opportunity to dive in the hero's head? To experience a sex scene from his point of view? To be able to show the reader how different he thinks from the heroine?

One of my favorite things to do is break down a scene and write it from both the hero and heroine's perspective. It's such a fun way to show the reader how men and women have different stakes, and experience different emotions.

I love getting into my hero's head. It gives me a giddy feeling that only third person POV can give.

Think about the tropes you particularly hate? Would it be a challenge to pick one you dislike, twist it up, and write it into your next story?

Chapter Fifty

The One Thing You Need to Know About Writing Character

Last night, I saw the movie *The Life of Chuck* directed by Mike Flanagan.

I'm a huge Flanagan fan, and an even bigger Stephen King fan. The movie was based on the short story included in If It Bleeds. Flanagan is known for his amazing horror movies so I was surprised when he decided to take this project on, but I was looking forward to seeing how he'd wrap his own vision in King's story.

I loved it. The movie is a quiet unfolding, told in sections that are given to the viewer non consecutively. There's a bit of a mystery. It was bittersweet and entertaining and layered with emotions that have been slowly unfolding even after I finished.

Watching movies, for me, is a way I inspire my own writing. I'm fascinated and obsessed with story in all formats, so a good television series or two-hour movie allows me to have fun, relax, yet still subconsciously work.

There are no spoilers so you can keep reading if you want to see the movie!

The most important scene was simple, yet I can't stop thinking about it. A businessman was walking along a busy street in a small town. There's a drummer set up on the corner who's playing. As he approaches, she spins into a different beat, and the businessman pauses. Slowly sets down his briefcase. And begins to dance.

I'm not saying more because I don't want to ruin the experience. It's a simple scene. Could be a bit cheesy if not done right. Yet, the impact of watching this buttoned up business person stop his automatic routine to break into dance in front of a crowd was startling, and enlightening. It made me smile. It made me tear up.

Because it is another reminder nothing is what it seems. People are not what they seem. We hurry along in life, passing strangers, saying we're okay with a polite or enthusiastic smile. We are people pleasers, people haters, but hoard our secrets and layers so deep, only our most intimate circle knows what's inside. And sometimes, not even them.

A memory can cause a flood; a memory from the past as a child; some good and some bad. It reconnects us with our humanness and if we stripped away all of our roles and surfaces, we'd all be pretty much…

The same.

We are people who not only laughed or cried but danced. Or created art. Or wrote words. Or played in the dirt. Or made sand castles at the beach. Or climbed trees to the tippy top so we could look down on the world. Most of us remember what it was like to be truly free, truly ourselves, whether it was a fleeting moment, a day, a week, a month. A summer.

Or through a two-hour movie. Or a book that made us remember.

If we took the time to stop rushing past and have actual conversations; to ask deep questions; there are discoveries to be found.

There are businessmen who remember how much they really loved to dance.

I remember when my son came back from senior prom. He told me he did the worm in a dance contest and flopped around on the floor because he was really bad at it. My jaw unhinged as the horror of the story hit me all at once. "Did everyone laugh at you?" I asked, already going to comfort him. "Did you stop and run out? Did your friends support you?"

My questions made him laugh and look at me like I had two heads. "Umm, no. I sucked but it was fun. What do I care if they laugh?"

I was stunned. Confused. In my world, in my mind, you didn't do things that may embarrass you in public or make people point and laugh. But that was my perspective. My son didn't give a shit. He just wanted to dance.

Is there a moment that hits us where we suddenly crave to get back in touch with that hidden part of ourselves? The one that gives joy without shame or apology?

What if next time, we put down our briefcase and…dance? In the street. In front of people. And not give a shit?

Would we reclaim something once lost?

That's how it is when we write a book. We are putting it all out on the page, into the world, without apology.

That's how you need to approach and write character. There are no easy answers so go deeper. If your character were to do something out of character, what would it be? What would they dream about? What was once alive in youth or the past and is now hidden?

If we hold the space, if we ask questions, we find so much more underneath. That's the good stuff.

Thanks to Stephen King and Mike Flanagan for this post. I'm looking at the world differently today and reminding myself to do one thing as I write my story today.

Make my characters dance.

Chapter Fifty-One

Post on The Writing Retreat

I RECENTLY READ a book I adored—a thriller called *The Writing Retreat* by Julie Bartz. It's been on my TBR for way too long, but I finally found my way to reading it.

I absolutely loved this book. It's the type of thriller that starts out one way, and morphs in a whole new direction I never saw coming. To pull off such a stunt takes writing chops, and I found myself shaking my head with admiration for the roller coaster ride.

But my favorite part of this book that I haven't been able to forget?

A certain scene that only writers can appreciate.

A scene that made me laugh and cheer in my head—maybe even out loud.

The scene was a speech made by the main character and the lead-up to it was brilliant and intricate. Here's the dialogue from the book, with no spoilers included:

"…I have this ability, to create whole worlds inside me…For so long I let other people make me feel like that wasn't good enough," I said. "That, in order to be a real writer, I had to get some agent or publisher to believe in me. Until then it would just be a delusion. But that's bullshit. Because even if I never publish anything, I'm a writer." I paused to take a breath. "I'm a writer, and no one can take that away from me."

Hell, yes.

How often do we forget our power? That we take blank space and create people who become real? That we have the guts to say we matter enough to share our vision with the world? That we are truly the magicians surrounded by the Matrix, who try and make order and sense and shove it all in a box so it can be tolerated?

God, I loved that speech. It's what I drill over and over in my book and course, *Write Naked*.

Write Free

We are writers because we write.

Nothing more, nothing less. It is why I tell young people they are already writers when they struggle to put words on the page, hoping and praying they gain some validity.

Writing gives you all the validity you will ever need.

We have to remember. It's so easy to forget; in a room; alone.

But the reminders and clues are there. I found one today reading a fictional thriller for entertainment.

They are always there; holding our hand; our creative mentors or spirits or energy guiding us forward and helping us fight.

Writing is power. Let's use it.

Chapter Fifty-Two

How to Rebuild Your Writing Nest

I SHOULD BE WRITING, but instead, I'm watching birds.

Specifically, the bird house attached to my back deck. Each season, I look forward to April because I know there will be new babies coming. Usually, the pregnant robins begin to check it out and poke around, trying to decide if they want to start their family by my sliding glass doors.

The nest is already there. I was surprised in the Fall when a sparrow discovered it and decided to stay instead of flying south –I don't know much about birds—settling in to the nest that had once housed baby robins.

She was a little thing, and before long, she'd decided to build the nest so high, you couldn't see anything behind the crazed sprawl of twigs and sticks. Sometimes, I'd try to peer in to make sure she was okay and still there, and I'd get an angry noise or she'd fly out, all pissy.

I'm not sure when she left. Sometime in the winter, the nest was empty again. So, I waited for Spring.

This week, it's finally happening. There were robins jumping around my back yard and I figured one of them would claim it. Imagine my surprise when more sparrows showed up, but this time, it was three of them. Somehow, they claimed the nest. How is that done, I wonder? Is it a matter of getting there first – like early birds get the worm? Is there a bird battle with a declared winner?

Today, I was mesmerized by the ritual of how they are readying the nest. It seems the last sparrow had made a mess, so the new sparrows are cleaning it up. Each of them takes turns rooting around and removing one twig at a time. It's fascinating—this strange sort of assembly line that's slowly lowering the high wall. Then one of the birds will climb into it and just stay there for a while, maybe testing it out. My deck is littered with nest materials.

Thank goodness, my dogs don't seem to bother or care about our returning visitors.

As I spent too much time watching this little nature miracle occur and ignoring my book, I allowed myself to simply enjoy the process of birds making a home. How often am I reminded that all of these tasks build toward the goal? Completing the small, sometimes boring tasks is a huge part of reaching the goal. Sometimes, I like doing them. Mostly, I don't. I believe these jobs should all try to be enjoyed, or at least, tolerated without unnecessary stress.

The birds look focused and happy. I'm sure some of the process is harder than other parts. Like writing a book. I find myself willing my Muse to get to the sixty percent mark where everything clicks and makes sense and suddenly, I'm flying, chasing the ending, giddy with the power of creativity and the knowledge the end is finally coming.

I still dread the early middle. It's the time I seek out reality television and lots of whining. Some books fare better than others, but I've rarely hit the hard parts and been happy. Yet, there will always be a middle to get through. Wouldn't it be wonderful next time, not to worry as much? To trust the slow slog, the questioning, the puzzle of what piece fits where? I have enough books behind me to call onto blind faith, but is there any other career where no matter how much you practice, you still think you can't do it?

I'd love to write one-hundred books by the end of my lifetime. That would be pretty damn cool. I think I'll have a giant party somewhere fun, with lots of food and wine and dancing. I'll invite family, friends, and readers. Anyone who wants to come. I have about forty books left to get there with no idea how much time I have left.

But I know one thing I'm always working on lately.

Not stressing as much during the hard parts.

Same with money. There is always a reason to worry about money and not having enough. Not making enough book sales. Not making enough royalty checks. Not getting enough contracts. Not having enough followers or subscribers. Not having movie or television deals. Not having all that I want and dream of.

Honestly? It will never be enough. I think if I got a Reese book pick and a feature film, I'd still worry about what's next. Or if I could even produce something good enough to be next. I'd want more—to push myself to the next level. It's a beautiful thing until it's not.

The key is balance. The delicate balance between growth and ego; between success and my asshole brain's idea of failure.

I've been doing a hell of a lot of work with manifestation and energy to try and smooth out those rough, bumpy edges.

I make more conscious decisions now to drill down and try to enjoy each task, in each process.

Even this week, I found myself rushing to an ending. I'm working on a proposal for a new book as I write this one that's coming out on Labor Day. As I switch back and forth, trying to create the perfect hook, blurb, rough outline, and a sample chapter, I'm feeling both the rush of writing something new with the devil on my shoulder whispering, "Faster. The sooner we get this done, the sooner we can get to the next thing!"

The unending tasks to be a successful writer nowadays is overwhelming. But each path is littered with tasks, many of them dull. Tweak ads. Post a video. Write a bonus short. Update back matter. Promote. Do a podcast.

Yet, each is important because it's a snowball effect, and leads to the entire snowman, outfit with hat, pipe, and hopefully yelling "Happy Birthday!"

Amy McNee wrote a wonderful post about rest that lit up my insides. Read it here:

She also wrote a beautiful book called We Need Your Art that's a fabulous read and perfect gift for any creatives. I like the way she's brave about sharing things we've always kept secret. When I wrote my book, *Write Naked*, I had a panic attack about revealing so many of my vulnerabilities in a world where I tried to be fabulous. It was not only the best experience but I became addicted to trying to help and share more for writers.

So, for now, I'm nesting. Fixing and fiddling with things on my desk. Words on the page. Various stories. Figuring out where I want to be next. Letting my Muse have her time to just be, until she's forging ahead, hungry for the next story.

It's all work. It all goes into the bigger goal. I wonder, if more of us had permission to just do less and let be, I bet the universe would sweep in, catch us up in a wave, and show us even more wonderful successful things because we finally gave it all up.

I'm ready now for the ride.

Chapter Fifty-Three

Lessons Learned from Italy

I VISITED ITALY RECENTLY, and felt like I was coming home.

There are certain places in the world where we end up and our soul sighs; a recognition and peace settle over you, as if you were there before. Cape May is a small beach town at the tip of the Jersey shore I travel to regularly that feels like this. So is Italy.

My son is currently studying abroad for college in Florence. Since my other son is a senior in high school, I decided to take him out of school early to can embark on a family trip. And though the travel was rough—a nine hour plane ride, two-hour train rides, JFK traffic, delays, long walks to the hotel dragging oversize luggage—it was worth it.

Florence is a city stuffed with art and history; a zig zag of narrow cobblestone streets that lead to hidden delights that would take a lifetime to explore. Our hotel was right by the massive Duomo, a giant gorgeous cathedral that seemed to overtake the horizon no matter where you looked. It was our true north and the direction that pointed to our temporary home.

I hadn't seen my son in three months—the longest I've been without him. As he greeted us at the train station, emotion overwhelmed me. How had he changed and grown so much without me? He emanated an easy confidence I hadn't seen before. His clothes were more stylish. He'd gotten taller, I swear! It was a joy and bittersweet to watch your child thrive away from you and I'm so grateful he worked hard to contend for one of the spots overseas to study film.

We had some adventurous experiences while we were there. We drove Vespas through the Chianti vineyards, speeding over rolling hills while the gorgeous scenery dropped us right into a movie or romance novel.

Just like the scene in my book, *The Secret Love Letters of Olivia Moretti*!

We drank wine in a castle and visited an olive oil farm. (*To Sicily with Love*)

We visited Venice and drifted down the canals in a gondola. (*Our Italian Summer*)

We headed to Pisa and Lucca, and immersed ourselves in exploring trattorias and unique shops filled with curated items, taking breaks for pizza and wine. (*A Wedding in Lake Como*)

But most of all, we resettled into simply being a family having fun. Sharing experiences we'd never forget. Laughing at the ups and downs and in betweens of travel.

It poured rain one day and we ended up splashing in puddles and getting drenched while visiting a chocolate festival. We bought an extra umbrella from a vendor, then got feasted on truffles that melted and danced in our mouth. We sought shelter in a dark pub that was also a record store, eating pizza and drinking wine.

My son showed us the famous window where he got melons thrown at him for talking too loud in the square at night. Yes, it seems my family heritage of Italians can be a cranky bunch with young Americans, but even worse? It happened while I was on the phone with him, and then again two weeks later. He now avoids that spot when talking on the phone to his family and friends too late at night. He posed for a picture in a comic parody underneath that window with his arms held out!

The week passed much too fast, but when I arrived back home, tucked away in my safe office where I spend the bulk of my time, I, too, was changed.

Experiences do that. In order to be the best type of writers, we need to venture out for those adventures.

What did I learn to bring back to the office?

Don't Plan Everything. Half of the fun was getting into messes, figuring stuff out, and laughing. We almost missed our train because we couldn't figure out the platform situation. My husband's luggage wheel fell off from the crooked pavement and then it wouldn't fit in the elevator so he had to drag it up three flights of stairs.

Things don't have to be perfect but we figure them out. Some are learning lessons. Other moments add to our life story—like discovering my son had done some questionable things one night at a bar with his friends. I wasn't happy but the story was hysterical. I'm still giggling even as I disciplined. Hearing about it at the scene of the crime was so much better than hearing years later at a holiday dinner!

We stumbled on the best shops and gelato by chance. Plans are great, but sometimes ditching them is even better.

Pay Attention: This is one of my lessons I teach new writers over and over. Travel is about paying attention because everything is new. But if you bring that child's mind back to the page? Your stories will shine brighter. You will be ready to handle surprise characters, plot twists, blocks, and stumbling. Attention is not only critical nowadays in this time of AI and endless scrolling—it's needed to see the bigger picture.

I didn't duck my head and bury myself in my phone when I was away. Videos and pics were great, but I didn't allow them to be my experience. Most of the time, I sensed it was more powerful to experience things in the moment then record them forever.

Why?

Because it makes it that much more precious. You can't hold it forever, just like a beautiful moment. Let's be in it more rather than a witness behind a phone camera.

Be Grateful: Yep, isn't it awful I threw this one in? Like #blessed. But honestly? It's the truth. It's important for a reason. I saw sights that brought tears to my eyes. While we were riding Vestas together as stunning scenery rolled by us, my heart actually hurt. I threw up a prayer of gratitude. I thought: my life is insane.

But guess what? I also remember thinking the same thing when I had no money, and my kids were in diapers, and we managed to save endlessly to go to Sesame Street Place for the day. They ate overpriced chicken fingers on Elmo plates and we got sunburnt watching the parade but all I remember is feeling giddy that I got to be with Big Bird and my boys.

I recognize how lucky I am all the time—even with the hard stuff. And believe me, bad shit happens to everyone. We all take our turns. This isn't some woo woo fake be grateful speech. Because I'm telling you it really works. It raises our energy and makes life better.

Write Free

Writing is hard, and this career is hard, and trying to make a living writing is really hard, but I'm grateful because I no longer have to do customer service insurance and get yelled at people and drive four hours a day while studying for my master's degree and having two babies.

God. I'm so grateful.

That's it. I'm off to write and dream about Italy. Hopefully my son won't be hit with a melon this week.

Chapter Fifty-Four

When Your Dreams Don't Match Reality

I HAVE BIG DREAMS.

I always have, even when I was young. I'd stare out the window, dreamily imagining my amazing life where I had fame as a writer, money, a passionate love, and this fab wardrobe. Many images showed me walking to some jet in my designer shoes holding my leather suitcase, off to a big book signing.

Yeah. LMAO.

Even when people tried to reign me in with reality, no one was going to get into my head and take my dreams away.

And I'm glad. Dreams are not only precious, but needed in a harsh reality. Dreams help us take risks and reach for something more. Something bigger that's unseen and invisible. Like faith.

But sometimes, I must admit my big dreams frustrate me because they simply don't match my reality.

For instance, right now I have this wonderful opportunity to pick what project comes next. I've spent time working on proposals, flirting with various stories, and sifting through the possibilities. Beyond the writing, I want to do all the things. I'm excited about getting my books on some new direct sites, reader apps, and audio. I want to run ads to my direct store, create amazing book boxes for my new book, and spoil my Ream members with lots of stories and new material.

I finally launched my Kickstarter for this book (yay!) and my first official writing course, *Write Naked*. It took endless time to research, plan, film, edit, and be brave enough to try and launch.

This is all great stuff, especially when I feel motivated and healthy instead of overwhelmed. Right now, all of these work dreams are taking a back seat to family matters. I have a graduating high school senior, award banquets, end of school events, track sectionals, and endless other things to take care of. I also recognize my boys will both be off to school in August and I will have to deal with an empty nest syndrome. Since I'll be able to work nonstop, I'm choosing to spend my precious time with my boys, having adventures, relaxing, and just bonding. That time is precious and I will never get this back again.

But my dazzling, shiny new projects? There is simply not enough time to do them all. Even without children, there are always distractions in our lives that keep us from rushing ahead without looking behind. Sometimes, I feel like my body is shaking and fiery with the need to write everything I can. To create in big, bold colors the world has never seen before. To take up a lot of space.

I want to work on my Christmas story. My new romcom. My spicy dark romance. And my weird, literary, kind of women's fic I'm obsessed with.

But the reality? I have to finish my current book, Covet, so it's ready to pub for September. I'm only at 30K so I have to push to finish this up by end of June with all these other distractions. I keep switching back and forth to work on the course and my fiction writing.

Write Free

And then it happened.

In the car, I got this idea for a cool new book that is so good, it blasted me like a missile and I hurried home to write the bare bones before it disappeared from my Swiss Cheese brain.

There's just one big problem.

I have no time to write it.

I don't want to wait! I want to dive into the deep end of the pool with this exciting, fresh story and be taken away from the mess—which is the slow, hard process of getting through my current rough draft that's taking me longer than I originally thought.

The funniest part? The days I actually have completely free to just sit in my office and become happily fossilized by endless hours of work?

I don't get much done. I end up putting out fires or wasting time doing silly things that don't move me forward. Then I get so mad and frustrated I owned these precious hours and didn't write all the words.

Years ago, this pattern would devastate me. I'd ping pong back and forth between frustration, anger, and depression. I'd say mean things to myself. None of it helped. None of the mental beatings got more words on the page.

Today, I've recognized this burning need to create all the things while my true reality completely contradicts it. I remind myself I'm choosing to spend my time elsewhere. Somewhere I deem just as important. After writing down all the pieces of my new book idea, instead of spinning out from not able to dive in, I made myself laugh out loud.

Why?

Because I'd rather have too many ideas and giant dreams and big-ass faith in the universe boomeranging me with some amazing opportunities than feeling blocked and empty.

Which has happened before, too.

Practice and time invested does help in this writing career. We learn it's all there waiting for us on the other side. We learn even though it feels like we can't write another book again, we will. We do.

I love the book Big Magic by Elizabeth Gilbert, who dives into the peculiarities and magical elements of the Muse and creativity.

What I wish for? To have endless, infinite time to follow every brilliant idea I have. To write every book in a matter of a few weeks and have it come out beautiful. To experience no boredom or drudgery or frustration while I'm writing my current book. That sounds wonderful, right? Write happily, perfectly, finish, rinse and repeat.

Too bad it's never gonna happen. To any of us. At least, not all the time, with every single project.

For now, I'm going to reset. Trudge word by word and get a chapter written of Covet. I'm going to show up for the work. I will let my Muse dream and plan and conspire for later. I tucked my proposal into my Dropbox folder with a longing sigh, knowing I'll write it one day.

Just not now.

But like my big dreams, it's always with me; waiting for the perfect time to appear.

Chapter Fifty-Five

Musicals, Movies, and the Magic of Story Structure

I LOVE NOT ONLY GETTING LOST in a story, but analyzing it as a writer.

I'm a huge television and movie buff. Back in the dinosaur days, my family had no money, so the big treat in our life was heading to the movies (many times in the heat of summer because we had no air conditioning). Drive-ins were probably some of the most exciting moments in my memory—pajamas, popcorn, endless mosquitoes, and those bulky speakers stuck in our crank car windows, letting in even more bugs. That's where I saw Jaws for the first time, which promptly ruined me. I literally refused to go into the deep end at my friend's pool. True story.

This past week, I went to see Superman. I loved it. How could you not with Krypto the rescue dog stealing the show? It reminded me of the vintage Superman movies—goofy in parts, with a Lex Luthor villain who absolutely stole the spotlight. I left the theater with my boys, chattering excitedly, then headed to the diner to keep the conversation going.

I also took my son into the city to see Hadestown. He's a writer, too, with big dreams of becoming a screenwriter and studying film in college. As the only two in the household who love musicals, we made a date and traveled in for a matinee. I knew it had won a Tony for Best Musical, but I had no clue what it was about. We went in blind—and I'm so glad we did.

Based on Greek mythology, Hadestown gives a modern twist to the stories of Persephone and Hades, and Orpheus and Eurydice. It was incredible. And two themes stuck with me and my son, long after the lights dimmed:

The story always repeats, caught in a vicious cycle, over and over again.

Don't look back.

Cryptic, right? I won't spoil it for you. But I will say this: every time I walk out of a well-crafted show, movie, or book, I come out changed. Even if just a little.

That's what an artist can do.

That's what we do—by showing up every day.

Even if it's a mess.

Even if it's a first draft.

Even if it's already "been done."

Let's integrate what I learned from Hadestown.

Lean on inspiration everywhere you look, not with the eagle-eyed gaze of a student learning a lecture for a test, but the curious, relaxed observer open to anything the world wishes to show you.

Ask for more. Demand more. From your career, your books, and yourself.

A book is written in a pattern, over and over. It can be termed a vicious cycle or an exciting ride that keeps looping to new destinations. The structure needs to be solid to build the rest. Study the core tools: GMC, the hero's journey, tropes, hooks, deep POV, and character ARC.

Then use your creativity to expand and stamp your fingerprint within the story.

We need to stop being ingrained in the past. Some feel like it was the good old days—the gold rush—our very own Camelot when the world was ours for the taking in this industry.

Don't get caught looking back. Be in the present. Plan and dream for the future. Accept what is, then twist to suit your needs.

Use all these tools to create the writing career suited for you.

Chapter Fifty-Six

The Art of Capturing Attention

I AM one of many subscribers to Emma Gannon's Substack *The Hyphen*.

She does a round up every other Sunday with interesting links, directing her readers to a variety of discussions, essays, posts, books, programs etc. Today, I clicked on the Ted Talk with Substack's Hamish McKenzie. It's worth a watch.

Hamish goes over the changes in media and where he thinks we are now. He discusses the concept of a media garden.

As I was drinking coffee and catching up on my lovely Substack reading, I kept going back to this Ted Talk and experiencing some real aha moments. As my thoughts spun, I decided to create a post on my reactions and ponderings on the topic of attention in the media landscape.

Especially with our books.

I've been unhappy with social media for a while. It's important I'm there for my work and connecting with my audience, but I feel like a turtle many times, wanting to shrink back into my shell and keep the quiet peace. There's so much noise everywhere. It's like going to a rock concert and experiencing the hours of loud ringing in my ears from the aftermath. Except this concert goes on and on.

Because the name of the game seems to be grabbing someone's attention.

Whether it's Booktok or ads or Reelz or YouTube shorts, we are told over and over that we have few seconds to capture another person's attention. If we don't, they will not buy our book. They will not read our book. They will not purchase our class. They will not read our newsletters. They will not care, and therefore, we will fail to sell ourselves and our products.

God, that's a lot of pressure to consistently perform.

Authors create under a spell of fear, chasing authenticity and using big words to pretend we know how to connect in order to properly brand ourselves. I am guilty of going down the portal – hell, I teach this concept in many of my workshops for a damn good reason. After all, every article tells me over and over to use action, from our videos to our first page, first chapter, ad headlines, captions, etc.

We discuss authenticity and trust, throwing these words around, but what does it really mean if we dive deeper? What really captures our long-term attention?

I believe it's connection. A feeling of trust from a creator who seems real. Receiving value without being sold value.

I'm about to say a bold statement.

I think we are wrong to cater to one's consistent inattention in the world. To produce faster, to film quicker, to speed up everything with hook lines and clickbait and be told there is one best way in this current culture to be noticed.

What's that one way? Make your content pop and hit hard. Be on brand. Make someone need to click the damn button to buy or read or watch.

This is why so many of us hate going online. We are heartbroken. Spiritually ill from the fakeness disguised as authenticity. We crave quiet and soft. We want deep meaning and slow thoughts. We need a damn break from the speed of everything exploding around us.

We don't need more of it.

It's another reason Substack has done so well. Connecting one on one to individual artists and writers is a slower, more meaningful process than scrolling and clicking on endless videos and ads for quick hits.

I was thinking about one of my books I wrote years ago called, *All Roads Lead to You*. I specifically remember doing a podcast with another author to celebrate the release. She asked me to read the first few pages of my first chapter for listeners. After I read it, I realized my first chapter was not an example of what I'd normally teach a new writer to do. It didn't grab attention. It didn't begin with action or a hook or create tension that would force a reader to need more. It didn't show the hero and heroine together and immediately get romance on the page. I would not read this if I was trying to show another writer the best way to open a first chapter.

The scene was quiet. My heroine woke up early, brewed coffee, and sat with her many rescue animals, pondering her thoughts, gazing at the sunset. She sensed something was coming but didn't know what it was. That's it.

When I finished reading, I actually apologized to the author. I said, "I'm sorry, that was a much slower beginning than I remembered." I was sheepish. A bit embarrassed. Yes, it was written well, but I doubted any new readers would sit up and go to buy my book immediately.

Her response was a game changer. "No, I actually loved it. The scene was quiet; it gave me time to ponder your character and warm up to the story. I pictured my own self, sipping coffee, petting my cat, ready for another day and what was to come."

I was so grateful. But it was much later I wondered why I'd felt the need to apologize for writing something slow and gentle. When had we lost the art of just letting things slowly unfold? Of taking our eighteenth slow breath – not our first? Or second?

I began writing on Substack because I wanted to write more posts where I can be thoughtful, give writers a nice place to ponder, and share my world.

My stories. How I see life. It has nothing to do with not wanting to make a profit with your work, but how you show up.

What if that same subscriber who sees your posts regularly, without pressure or force, organically drops in to read your work? What if your fans come in a slow trickle rather than a flood, and stay because they really want to be there?

I like the image of that world. Especially as I age, in both years and my career, and find I don't want to push endless books out anymore without intentional thought.

I think the world needs more content that moves in languid, relaxed steps. No getting to the action right away. No intense shockers to force people to find out what happens next. I still love a good thriller or a book full of plot twists. But we don't need them all the time. There is space, especially now, for a gentle unfurling of content in order to create connection, and cement attention.

Maybe the world needs more opening chapters that offer us a seat, a cup of coffee, a cozy blanket, and an animal to pet. Maybe we need to be challenged in the exact opposite way – to wait and see what happens. What does that space look like in author branding and our books?

Yes, maybe less money? Less sales? Less curious eyeballs on our work? But still, this need beats within me, and I think I will begin to chase it. See how it unfolds in my stories and media content and articles. Explore with childlike curiosity. Walk instead of run.

I will go slowly and see.

Chapter Fifty-Seven

The Art of Holding Back

LAST WEEK, I was in Cape May on the beach. I watched as two overgrown puppies bounded across the sound and played in the waves. They wore bright pink vests. Their ears flopped as they chased each other. Their mom and dad watched, laughing, obviously in love with their new additions.

The water sparkled and sunlight touched the tips of the waves, exploding into a frisson of light. I sat in my low-rise beach chair with my toes buried in the sand and watched the dogs swim. The sun was hot, but a gentle breeze relieved the sting of my newly burnt skin. The air smelled of salt and sweat; of sun and summer. A Kindle was gripped in my hand. The clouds blurred with the line of ocean and sky and merged into one.

It was an endlessly perfect moment, never to be captured again. I tried to cling to every detail and shove it deep into my memory to capture the emotion.

Would I forget it, though? I asked myself. Should I grab my phone and record a video so it will be registered on my FB memory feed years later? Should I share on my subscription or Substack or Threads or IG? Can I squash it into a neat package for others to consume and like and share?

I sat on the hard bleachers, amidst crowds of families, forgetting my back ached after sitting for almost two hours. My lips curved into a smile so big and wide, my face hurt. I watched my son as he stood on stage and delivered the Valedictorian address to his graduating high school class. He looked handsome in a royal blue robe, with multiple medals adorning his neck. The cap perched on his head and covered up the too-short haircut he'd gotten for the occasion.

He spoke without hesitation, confident in his words. Tears burned my eyes. I've never been more grateful and proud of this beautiful boy I got to raise—this boy who owned my heart and had his own story to tell the world. It was his last chapter in a book I'd begun to write with his birth, and now it was time to let go. The emotions choked my throat; the dying sunlight attacked my vision; sweat pooled down my back; and people crushed together in unity for a brief event that was almost holy with importance.

I asked someone to video the speech so I didn't have to watch him through my camera. I hung on to every word my son spoke. I lived and breathed that moment.

Later that night, everyone uploaded their graduation videos and pics and it was a beautiful thing to watch.

I didn't. In fact, I didn't share anything until days later, when people began bugging me and my husband asked me several times why I hadn't posted such an amazing event for my friends to see.

And the voice whispered quietly.

Because that moment belonged to me.

Soon, I'd give it away, but I wanted to greedily treasure it for a bit longer.

What do perfect moments really mean?

We've begun to slowly erode those types of moments in our pursuit of sharing, authenticity, or recruiting witnesses to our lives. Many of us are trying really hard to enjoy the unfolding of cool things but also record for prosperity – in either likes, money, or relevancy.

These types of directed thoughts live beneath the surface of our brains. It's not like we stop before posting to ask ourselves why we really want to share something.

We are simply trained now to record all our moments.

This can be a problem.

We cannot give away all parts of ourselves. Some memories or moments should be selfishly kept in our heart and bodies, secreted where no one else can find them. Especially to strangers, though they are tagged as friends on our social media threads.

Sometimes, it's much more powerful to be and contemplate how those moments made us feel. To pull up those memories when we need them, usually when we are quiet or something makes us remember the past.

There is nothing wrong with sharing.

There is also nothing wrong with not sharing.

I've been doing more conscious not sharing. I went to a Rob Thomas concert with my bestie. Rob Thomas is one of my fave artists of all times, excluding Taylor. We wore matching shirts and drank wine out of plastic cups and danced our asses off as Rob sang our favorite lyrics. I teared up with joy at such a perfect moment. I shot a few videos and snapped pics but not many. I wanted to simply enjoy myself.

When I got back to the hotel, I didn't post.

When I got back home, I didn't post.

My friend did. She tagged me, which is fine. Great for memories later. But I realized it was a night I didn't want to give away to anyone. I still had his music singing in my head. I wanted every precious second for myself. I wanted to own and devour the happiness I experienced.

As I pull back more and consciously decide what or when I want to share, I find posting days or weeks after the event passed is more enjoyable. I have time to process before releasing.

I've been digging deep to try and find why I'm so hesitant to put my life out there. I do a lot of this for work. Helping writers by showing up and sharing my experience/lessons is important. Trying to get my books into reader's hands is important. Being part of community and giving back is important.

I was scrolling randomly on Notes and see so many posts with tons of likes and reshares. Many are encouraging. Some are quotes or writing about a vulnerable moment. Others are clips of a thought or a needy request to connect with others, or seek encouragement. From the bulk of responses, it's nice to see how many people want to help.

This is nice. People need more feel-good things to like and read. But the sheer volume of comments in my feed made me pause before throwing my own stuff out there.

I wondered about my own intentions in my quest to share and be a part of everyone's feed. Am I looking for proof my thoughts are important? Am I looking for more followers? Am I looking to be liked and therefore, the more attention to the post, the more valued I feel?

Kind of deep, I know. But a good thing for me to ponder. Being a 9 on the Enneagram, I lean heavily into wanting to give, and having people like me without a shred of conflict.

Hard to do if you want to write what you want and being naked in front of everyone with your stories.

But for me, books are different. That's the place I like to bare it all. To dump all the mess and emotion and thoughts and feelings onto the page and into the story.

Not on social media. At least, not all the time.

I have now given myself permission to keep my perfect moments private when I want without judgement. Without wondering if I'm missing out on a big opportunity to share and be authentic and try to connect with readers and writers.

When I do post, it's usually on impulse, or because I really want to put it out in the world. Not feel like I should.

Let's keep some of our moments to ourselves. Let's be quieter and more contemplative of those times and not reach for the phone. Let's not try to caption our emotions of the moment with smart hashtags littered with keywords. Let's not go to see who liked it or cared enough to stop their scroll.

Even better?

Let's keep it all for our stories.

Chapter Fifty-Eight

Three Lessons I Brought Home from Hawaii (Besides Jet Lag)

I MISSED the tsunami evacuation on Waikiki by hours—which affected the beach by our hotel—and am so lucky to be home safe.

I was gone for ten days and didn't work. I always bring my laptop on vacation just in case, and I did use it—on the plane ride home, cramming in seven hours of catch-up instead of binge-watching movies or reading.

A summer trip normally wouldn't push me to write a post, but this time, I broke every rule that grounds me as a writer and businessperson.

I decided to launch a Kickstarter on August 1.

I have a book releasing September 3.

And… that book isn't finished.

It's a lot.

Somehow, I overshot. I planned from a dream schedule instead of my reality schedule. I didn't anticipate how intense it would be—graduation, my son's health issues, loss of college housing, a major trip, and about a thousand other things that hit all at once.

In that whirlwind, I told myself I could do it. I could finish the book. I could handle the Kickstarter. I'd make it all work.

Now? I'm not so sure.

The Kickstarter is launching. The book will be finished. But squeezing that much work into this tiny window feels like living in a genie bottle—cramped, breathless, claustrophobic. Instead of calmly writing a dozen campaign updates, I'm staring anxiously at my computer with jet lag, wondering if any of it is good.

Here's what I thought would happen with Kickstarter:

- Final approval? Check.
- 100 pre-launch followers? Working on it.

- Stretch rewards and early bird deals? Almost.
- A dozen written posts and a clear networking plan? Not even close.
- As for *Covet*, the first draft is done—but it's rough. I still need to:
- Rewrite
- Send it to the editor
- Fix again
- Finalize the paperback cover
- Upload all formats by August 21
- Market it.

Oh, and I'll be gone again next week on another long-planned trip. That shouldn't be a problem… if the dream schedule had worked out.

But instead, I'm working with reality. And as I write this post, I'm actually laughing—because this isn't new. I once rewrote an entire book in ten days and offered my children to the productivity gods in the process.

Somehow, things always get done. Not always perfectly. But they get done.

And today? That's enough.

Chapter Fifty-Nine

Three Things I Learned on Vacation

I RETURNED to my real life but am determined to bring some things home with me besides souvenirs and a sun-burn.

My first day back in my office, I took some time with a journal to free-write about those moments I felt truly free. I asked myself what I thought were some items I discovered that weighed me down when I was home.

These are the three things that came up.

1. **I read too many emails.**

I've always been the kind of person who jumps on email in the morning to get stuff done. But now it feels like another form of social media—a place where other people's input floods in and derails my focus. I'm reactive instead of intentional.

On vacation, I slowed down. I drank my coffee. I browsed only what brought me joy. And I realized: I'm subscribed to too much. So I started unsubscribing. I deleted things instead of saving them for "someday." It felt like freedom.

2. **Doing nothing is wildly productive**.

Sitting by the ocean—no book, no podcast, no conversation—was magic. My Muse finally exhaled and started whispering to me again, like a teenager suddenly ready to spill secrets.

And then... my kids. They wrestled in the waves and fought over tubes and made me laugh until I cried. I saw them again. Really saw them. The cowlick. The crooked grin. The way they run down sidewalks like they own the world. My heart burst seeing them be silly and free, before they're back off to college and real life hits them hard. For a little while, we were in a bubble and grateful to get there. Not many people can.

3. **Choosing no action is powerful**.

So many people tried to reach me while I was away. Things felt urgent. Decisions. Emails. Texts. But I didn't respond. I didn't explain. I didn't even apologize.

I did nothing.

And it felt revolutionary.

Not everything is truly urgent—it just feels urgent. By stepping away and choosing silence, I got my power back. I stopped living in constant reaction. And I remembered who I am.

This isn't a post to complain or vent. The truth is, the Kickstarter will go live. The book will be finished. I may write three posts instead of twelve. I may reach fewer people. I may run fewer ads.

But the time off was worth it.

Letting go of *perfect* might be the most productive thing I've done all summer.

Chapter Sixty

Five Things I Learned Writing To Sicily with Love

(Previously published on Chuck Wendig's blog, terribleminds.com)

WITH EACH BOOK I WRITE, I learn something new.

Sometimes, I like to take time to ponder and figure out the big lessons a book has taught me. *To Sicily with Love* was a big women's fiction book that challenged me to stretch and grow. I did a ton of research and this book took a long time to write. Here are some of my reflections:

1. **Trust your voice and process**

I've written over fifty books yet each time I start a new one, it's like learning to walk all over again. There aren't many jobs out there where you can continuously doubt yourself even with a string of successes behind you and proof you can actually do the damn thing. The creative process is truly janky, and mysterious, and kind of magical, so I've learned one thing that's like a rope line in a blinding snowstorm.

Trust.

When I started writing *To Sicily with Love* I felt completely overwhelmed. Out of my depth. I realized the book I pitched and sold featured a giant Sicilian family steeped in tradition and I had to not only construct a bunch of characters that leapt off the page, but make them all different, set in a culture I simply didn't know much about.

I also promised my editor the story would be lighthearted, even with the death of Aurora's mother, but damned if I didn't find myself in the muck of grief and darkness as my heroine found herself simply incapable of being her usual fabulous, goal-oriented self.

After a brief panic that I was delivering the exact book my editor didn't want, I relied on the only thing left. My trust to chase the story, no matter what emerged. So, I shut down the monkey mind whispering I could never do this right, and let my voice guide me through. I went to the dark places of regret, grief, and loneliness. When I got stuck in the details, instead of committing to my usual process of writing linear, I jumped around and wrote certain scenes that called to me. I blew up the secure, traditional way of creating a story and trusted with this book, I needed to do something different.

It worked.

Sometimes, you need to go in blind with a story and trust you will get there on your terms.

2. **Setting is a character.**

When I first began writing, I hated setting. I wanted to get straight to the good stuff, like dialogue and sex and action. But I realized as I wrote bigger and deeper novels, I needed to up my game. Setting is not just a background where your story takes place. If done well, it becomes another character, and can add an important element readers love.

I learned to slow down and pay attention. I learned to savor not only what I can see and describe, but the taste, feel, and scent of the world surrounding my characters. Readers want escape, and whether it's a spooky, dilapidated lodge in the mountains during a snowstorm, or the lush earthy hills of Tuscany, our job is to make our readers feel like they are there.

Setting shouldn't be a distraction from the story. It should be part of it. Whether you write about a cupcake festival in a quirky upstate farm or a six-course meal served at a crowded pine table with loud Italian relatives talking over one another, put me there. And please allow me to taste all the food.

Receiving endless letters from readers who tell me they got hungry reading my book, or planned a trip to Italy because of my story is the biggest payoff and worth all the work.

3. **Research your shit.**

It's so hard not to get lazy with research, unless you are a writer who loves it. For me, I don't mind a little, but with To Sicily with Love, I found myself in the deep end of the pool. I hadn't gone to Sicily. It took me forever to finally find the perfect town in Sicily for my setting, and I'd get frustrated after hours spent online with no new words.

But it's a critical part of process. In order to write the story well, I needed to know not only the surroundings of the town, but where people ate, how people made a living, how they thought and spoke within the small community. I refused to allow people who'd visited Sicily to read my book and find a bunch of errors or misinformation.

I put a call out to my readers asking who went to Sicily and if they had relatives there. I spoke with many on the phone, took endless notes, and pored over their pictures. I used maps, blog posts, videos, and watched everything I could find.

I learned the process of olive oil making. I learned about the fish market. I learned how jewelers make precious coral.

And all of this research led to rich, detailed scenes in the book that leapt from the page.

Research is a delicate balance. Use it to enhance the storyline, but be careful not to get so excited about what you learned, you throw in too much detail and drown the reader.

4. **Emotion is key.**

When my writing goes off course, as sometimes it does, I bring myself back to the most important element that drives every single book I write.

Emotion.

I can have the most gripping plot and fascinating characters, but if readers don't care, the story will be flat.

This means digging deep into a character's mind and dragging out all their secrets. What they want. What they fear. What they dream. And what they believe is getting in the way.

Goal, motivation and conflict needs to be wrapped up in emotion. A character behaving in an interesting way will remain flat on the page unless we dig deep underneath the skin and make them human.

With Aurora, after losing both her parents in tragic circumstances, her perfect life she was so proud of is blown up, leaving her doubting everything she thought she believed in. I needed to allow myself to revisit and process my own grief, depression, and roller coaster of emotion I experienced when I lost my dad. A writer needs to be brave to unearth their own monsters to give life to the characters.

It can be the difference between a good book, and a great book.

5. Use theme to create a better story

Theme is like the smoke that drifts from the pages of a story but is hard to grasp. I like to compare theme to a luscious gourmet meal, moving from appetizer to dessert. Theme makes a reader feel full and complete at the end of a book.

Themes can include elements such as family, friendship, second chances, home, betrayal, chaos, forgiveness—any big type of subjects we deal or struggle with in our lives. It can be broad or narrow.

I've used themes while planning my book and deciding what I wanted to explore. I've also written my entire book before realizing what my themes were. Then I go back and layer the scenes with that specific theme in mind. Books can begin with one planned destination, then lead to the wild unpaved paths one never intended. The surprises are a reason I love my work so much

When I began writing To Sicily with Love, I knew my themes in the book would be grief and forgiveness.

My heroine, Aurora, travels to Sicily and meets her grandfather, who had cut ties with Aurora's mother after she ran away to get married. Aurora resents him for abandoning her mom. He's gruff and curt, giving off the impression of non-caring. As the summer unfolds, they form a tentative bond, which deepens over time, mirroring the relationship between the grandfather and mother.

Both relationships from the past and present rely on forgiveness. Aurora must forgive her grandfather and mother. Her grandfather must forgive her mother. They must both forgive themselves for actions that led to regrets. It is a full circle of forgiveness, given to the reader within the relationships. It's played out with subtlety, threaded into each building scene and pulling the overarching pieces of the story together.

Digging into the theme you'd like to explore in your story is a vehicle to create a richer, more dynamic story.

Chapter Sixty-One

How I Got on TV and Publicity Insight from my Latest Release

Publicists have a hard job.

In this current world, it doesn't need just to bleed to lead. People nowadays require something so shocking and gory it resembles a horror movie, freezing us in place and transfixed to watch.

Since I watch horror but don't write it, that method won't work for me.

Instead, most authors are looking for help creating a pitch that's got an intriguing hook, fresh perspective, or holds current interest/trend. Since the market is glutted with books, this is another place where uniqueness comes in to help.

A book with a specific theme, setting, or subject is helpful. It's not enough anymore to tag your book the next Fourth Wing in romantasy and watch it soar. Tropes are everywhere. Bookstores now tout what they want to sell, not the publishers. Readers have an endless pick of sales and discounts.

It's extremely difficult to pick out what makes your book special and fight for space on podcasts, entertainment sites, social media, influencers, and other outlets that help spread the word about your book.

Many authors don't even work with a publicist. They may get an inhouse person assigned at trad, but with self-publishing, we're on our own or need to hire.

There's an array of companies to choose from, capable individuals, and a buffet of choices. But this post isn't about telling you who to pick, or if you should hire your own or not.

I simply wanted to pull back the curtain on this particular release, *The Reluctant Flirt*, and show how the pieces fell together. Each book I write has a different publicity plan. Sometimes, I hire. Sometimes, I collaborate and rely on my publisher.

Sometimes, I do a specific IG/TikTok tour. Sometimes, I do it all myself.

Let's go over the specs. *The Reluctant Flirt* is a spicy romcom and the second book in my Outer Banks series. It's third person POV.

My publisher is Blue Box Press. They hired Get Red PR to work with the book.

Both have a solid foundation and networking in the book world so I was well taken care of. There was an extensive IG and influencer tour with ARCS; Goodreads giveaways and reader letter spotlight; a feature in Netgalley; multiple digital ads in Goodreads and popular book sites; many podcast appearances, and curated book boxes pre-publication. Most ground was well covered.

Barnes & Noble also gave the book a special Nook edition. It was promoted to B&N customers for free for a month and included a reader letter, a bonus epilogue, different cover, and playlist. I also did a live appearance on Nook Press and Audrey Carlan interviewed me.

A month before *The Reluctant Flirt* released, we did a BookBub for the first book, *Book of the Month*. It was offered for free, and I signed up for a bunch of newsletters to support the BookBub.

This included E-reader news, ebooksoda, Written Word Media which included a bunch of specific newsletters, Freebooksy, and many others.

Book of the Month reached #1 on Amazon in the free category.

We had about 35K downloads.

I supported the release of *The Reluctant Flirt* with numerous newsletters shares with bestselling authors, Facebook ads, and social media.

These promotion efforts were spread out before launch, on release day, and through August.

When I got the email asking if I'd be able to go to the local TV station in Outer Banks to film a live interview, I was ridiculously excited and grateful. I'd done radio, podcasts, and every other type of event except TV. The morning show was called Coastal Live and highlighted the Outer Banks.

My publicist was able to spin my book into interest due to the setting. I leaned in heavily to Duck and Corolla, writing about the sea turtles, the wild horses, and many local spots of interest residents and visitors were interested in.

My years of writing experience, past books, and bestseller tag helped secure my spot. My publicist did a Zoom call with me where she helped me with specific questions, and prepped me to feel calm and knowledgeable.

The station held a cozy, local feel and everyone was incredibly kind. I was brought into a room to wait, while I chatted with another guest who was in not-for-profit healthcare. Then I was brought into the studio, where the host touched base with me and went over various questions he'd ask, and specific instructions on where to look.

I sat in a gray padded chair in my maxi dress (don't wear a short skirt because many chairs are high!), put on my cheerful smile, and kept my gaze on the host. Once I got going—I was super nervous at first—the rest came easily. It was simply another conversation I'd had with endless hosts before, and I was lucky I had some public speaking skills behind me.

It ran for only four minutes. When I was done, the host told me I was like a pro and that he'd love to have me in again for my next book. My husband took a bunch of pics, and then we were done.

The entire experience was wonderful. I was glad it wasn't for a big network because they gave me personal attention I needed.

The segment aired live and some friends were watching at the time. Then, the interview dropped on their website later that night, and I was able to link it and put it out everywhere.

Did it sell thousands of books?

No.

Did it sell hundreds of books?

No.

Did it solidify my author brand, and give my series another chance to reach readers?

Yes.

Was it an experience I'd never forget?

Yes.

I think it's important when doing any PR to have your expectations clear. Authors have gone on Good Morning America with minimum results in sales. Others have done smaller spots that gave them a viral wave of sales.

No one knows. Because after you've prepped, and gotten your amazing spot secured, it's also a matter of luck and timing.

The best way to do any PR is with a low-key positivity and knowledge you are doing everything possible to help your book succeed. Not desperate possible.

Hopeful possible.

After my tv spot, I signed at a local bookstore in Duck. I was excited because I'd featured that same bookstore in my series. My table was set up outside, in a small corner, and I didn't get a ton of traffic, even after promoting it on tv.

I sold ten books.

I met a fan who gushed and connected with me.

I met a few friends who were on vacay and they'd deliberately driven out to see me and get books.

Ten books for me isn't a great showing. It was a Thursday, extremely hot, and from 10am to Noon.

But…other great things happened.

I met the bookstore owner, who was a wonderful person I loved talking to. She owns two other bookstores and offered me another event opportunity to attend. She also said my books sold really well, so I signed all of the stock and she made arrangements to order even more. I now have a new contact in the book world.

Win/Win.

I've gone to book signings where I've spent hours and the line was wrapped around the block.

I've attended ones where it was packed, where it was empty, and everything in between.

I've learned to take each event individually and not judge. It all goes into the bucket of meeting readers, putting yourself out there, and giving your book the best opportunity you can.

My next book, Covet comes out in two weeks. It's a completely different type of book: angsty, new adult, and super steamy. I need to lean into new marketing strategies to reach that audience so I'll be experimenting. I'm treating the launch as a soft one. No high expectations or disappointments. My pre-orders aren't as high as I hoped. As the third book in a series of cliffhangers, I want to see how I can make the most money and where I should be targeting.

My Kickstarter is complete and I reached my goal of 10K to launch this book and my *Write Naked* course. This is an incredible result. Most

Write Free

Kickstarter campaigns in the publishing category never reach 10K. I also have a stable of new writers and readers I can bring into my world. For my third project on Kickstarter, I feel like I'm always learning new things to make the next one better.

Sometimes, it's a time for growth. I'm ready for it. Even the obstacles I know will always be there.

I remind myself that pain brings an even sweeter thrill of success and pride.

I am ready for both.

Chapter Sixty-Two

When You Hit #1 on Amazon

It's difficult out there in publishing.

I've seen a lot in my fifteen years writing full-time, but lately? I'm a bit overwhelmed at the squeeze in the industry and what it takes to get a book enough readers to make it move. A lot of the actions regularly used isn't working as well. Authors are pivoting in various ways, and trust me, this isn't a gloom and doom post, because amidst the difficult is more freedom for authors than we've ever had before.

Plenty are making money. Plenty are successful. Many are quietly successful, churning out books regularly, hitting their sales marks, and building a niche solid community.

The bottom line? I've learned to really savor the winning moments nowadays. There is no more expectation of success as I had before. So when I woke up this morning, and found *Book of the Month* sitting at the #1 spot in the entire Amazon store, I got a bit teary eyed.

Let me tell you what old me would've said:

The book is free. It better hit number one or you'd be a failure.

Well, you couldn't even make a dent with your last release, it's about time.

You paid enough and have a nice publisher behind you that made this happen.

Don't get too attached, it'll drop in the next hour and disappear completely…

Let me tell you what new me says:

I'm so proud of you! You love this book and now more people get to read it!

Look at what your team accomplished! What a blessing to reach new readers!

Who cares if it's there for an hour? You did it! You got the number one slot in the entire world!

I'm so damn grateful for this job, this book, this team, this career, my readers....

I always teach writers to celebrate wins. I wrote 3K yesterday and I gave myself a nice pep talk because I've been struggling with words recently. And it felt good. I like being nice to myself. I like being kind. My poor Muse and sensitive soul has been through enough self-discipline over the years and needs a softer approach.

I'm writing this post to celebrate my achievement but to also show again the major ups and downs of a long term career author. You never get THERE. You never stay THERE.

It's a long journey full of wonder and hidden roads and potholes and craters and sunshine and rain.

Just like life.

Author's Note: In Chapter 37, I wrote a post about my disappointment with sales for *Book of the*

Month. As you can see, months later, a BookBub lifted this novel to #1 on Amazon in the free category. This is proof you never know what will happen with a book in the future!

Chapter Sixty-Three

Burnout

AUTHOR BURNOUT IS NOW AN EPIDEMIC.

Years of rapid write and release and trying desperately to publish more books than our bodies are capable of, have led many authors to burnout.

What's burnout? Is the term being overused or thrown around for dramatic effect?

No. It's real and it's dangerous. Some authors I know have had such serious health and writing block issues, they cannot do anything for months. Some have stopped writing completely. Some get a day job. Some are struggling and paying for coaching to get back to a healthy state of mind with their creativity and ability to produce books.

I'm not an expert on getting an author through burnout so this post isn't meant to be a simple three steps to avoid burnout. Since I've also struggled and once spent four months in a chair with no energy to write anything, it's something I'm now aware of. Now, I look for it. I've learned the signs. I had to implement changes so I don't get there again.

It was hard. A simple bullet list won't cure it. But I will say these are a few things I learned that help me when I feel like I'm nearing the edge of the cliff. Usually, I peer over, see where I'll end up, and try to choose better options so I can step back.

Here they are:

Do more with less – take a break from writing new content. Lean on backlist to do some heavy hitting and change focus to lighter admin things that can bulk up profit. Realize it's not forever but if you don't pull back now, it will get worse. Like resting for a cold before it turns into pneumonia.

Write something completely different – brainstorm a pen name, write in a new genre, write in a new format, anything to bring some joy and freedom to what has now come a job and career that supports you. Journal or do morning pages and that's it.

Do nothing. Emma Gannon once was at the top tier of the writing and publishing industry and had a complete breakdown. She stopped working and did nothing for months. By changing her focus and not staying on the hamster wheel she discovered new passions, new ideas, and a new way to change her career. She wrote a little book called, *The Year of Nothing*, and another, *The Success Myth*. Reading them helped me.

Say no. You absolutely must strip down your life to necessities. Put a message on your email that you are unavailable – no explanation needed – and will return messages when able. Send more things to an assistant if you have one. Push out deadlines that are flexible. Say no to marketing events or conferences or signings. Say no to new offers and the never ending to do list. Say no to having lunch with people you don't like. Say no to chores and tasks that drain your energy. Say no to parties that make you feel like you'll cry if you're forced to go. This is temporary. You can be kind and still say no. Everyone will be waiting for your return to the world when you're in a better place.

Seek out things that make you happy:

There are certain podcasts or shows or books that simply make me happy or calm. Some have told me watching cooking shows or HGTV channel puts them in a relaxed state. Or listening to a familiar voice on a favorite podcast. This is the time to seek out these types of influences and nothing that will jar your mind or body.

Usually, the thing to avoid during this delicate period is: news and social media or people who truly trigger you. Your body needs soothing. It needs care. Your Muse needs to feel safe in order to create. I have been known to binge reality shows for a few days before I am able to finally get into my office. Or read for hours from my keeper shelf. Seek comfort in all its lovely forms.

Ask for Help:

This is the hardest for me because I do everything the best! But this is the time to lean on your assistant. Or authors to help promote your release. Or hire someone to do ads. Or look at that new course you've been needing to take and put it off till next year or next quarter.

It's amazing what happens when you end up unable to do tasks. Somehow, things fill in the void and life moves on. It's actually uncanny when you go back to the desk and realize life has moved on without you, but that you can pick up where you left off. Or even better? Pick up in a brand-new place.

I know money is usually the main concern, but if you go into burnout, you won't be able to do a thing. Treat it like your health. If symptoms are cropping up and the pain is increasing, seek treatment now rather than wait until it's too late.

Protect yourself and your precious Muse. You are worth it.

Do you feel like you're nearing burnout? If so, what steps can you take to help?

Chapter Sixty-Four

Cool Quotes

I FREEZE when someone asks what my favorite quote is.

Kind of like trying to name my favorite book. I love quotes. I have them littered all over my desk: some on sticky notes; some framed; some scribbled and tucked away so I discover them when needed.

I'm a quote junkie. I thought it would be fun to share some of my most cherished ones.

"Hold the space."

This is on a sticky note at my desk. It's a reminder to listen: really listen, not just wait for your turn to talk. And if someone is dumping some really hard stuff, it's a reminder to be quiet and hear them. Be with them. Sometimes, that's what anyone really wants – someone to sit with them in the dark.

"Trade your expectations for appreciation and your whole life will change."~ Tony Robbins.

Another quote on my desk. Every time I reach for gratitude in anything that happens to me, my perception of the event changes. This is powerful stuff and a daily practice.

"Protect the work"

Heard this from a speech by Susan Elizabeth Phillips. Another note in front of me so I always remember everything comes second to the work. If I need to get off social media or not read a bad review to protect my peace and Muse, I do it. My job is to make sure I do my best when I open my manuscript and sometimes that means shutting off other aspects of the world and my mind.

"Life happens for me, not to me."

A concept I heard from Tony Robbins but not sure who said the exact quote? This has been a game changer for me. Everything settles into a new perspective when I trust and believe that even the bad is good in some way. I just can't see why yet. I talk about this concept a lot in my course and my workshops because I believe if you are rejected from one thing, there is something better out there for you. We don't know the path we are meant to walk just as we don't know what will happen next on a blank page (unless you're a master plotter, lol!).

"Trade your expectations for appreciation and your whole life will change."

Yeah, another Tony Robbin's quote. I like his conferences! This is framed so I see it all the time. It's my thread toward gratitude and a daily reminder that everything is a gift. Yes, it's a practice. No, I don't get there all the time. I'm not supposed to—that's what practice means. I am kind to myself when I screw up. But when I'm in this mindset, I'm more productive and more joyful. That is my goal.

. . .

"Writing is something you do alone in the room."

~Michael Ventura

I've quoted this piece many times through the book because in its utter simplicity, the sentence invokes our entire lives. We must be okay to be alone for a very long time. Wrestling words from nothing, filling blank spaces with ideas, locking ourselves in this space—no matter how we decorate it—to be alone to write. We live many lives in that room. We fight monsters. We find joy. We find ourselves, if we are very lucky.

"Tomorrow may be hell, but today was a good writing day, and on the good writing days nothing else matters." *~Neil Gaiman*

For me, this is truth. On the days I've written well; written true and deep and authentic; I am at my most joyful. I am satisfied in that bone weariness many feel after a great workout. I am cleaned and pure. I am drained. So, I keep this to remind myself of why I'm writing that day. Because it's so much harder not to write.

. . .

Write Free

What are some of your favorite quotes? What do they make you feel about your life?

Chapter Sixty-Five

The End

I like typing the end.

I thought this was a good place to wrap up and share a few final musings.

As I finish this book, my boys are both in college. I'm struggling with empty nest, but a friend told me to change the phrase to bird launcher. After I laughed, I realized she was right. It made me feel good instead of sad. Perspective is everything.

I'm ready to dive into my 62nd book. I'm excited for new projects and to see what happens next. I want to continue to help authors in any way possible, which is why I also created a private Ream mastermind group. It's limited to only ten people though, so I can give everyone the time and care. We meet on Zoom once a month to discuss our goals and projects. If you're interested in joining, I have some slots left so check it out at: https://reamstories.com/jenniferprobst

You can also take my Write Naked course, which is a personal, deep dive into all things writing. It's me speaking with you one on one, and like this book, it's easy to dip in and out of modules as you'd like. You can check it out here: For Writers

www.jenniferprobst.com/for-writers

I wanted to thank everyone who helped bring this book into being, and supported my Kickstarter.

Here are some specific people who made a difference to me and this project:

Claire Taylor, Enneagram teacher and writer at The Liberated Writer; Russell Nohelty, author of Substack *The Author Stack*; Lee Savino, writer and founder of Millionaire Author Mastermind on Facebook; and to both for the invite to speak at The Six Figure Experiment podcast; Ines Johnson, writer of fiction and nonfiction at Substack's *Ines Johnson is Having a Breakdown.*

For my fellow authors who helped share in their

newsletters and on social media, my deepest thanks.

Thanks to Lauren Layne for making me this beautiful cover and being my friend. Thanks to Jennifer Jakes at the Killion Group for formatting and always taking my last-minute requests.

This tribe means the world to me. I wish you peace, and health; success and money; and most of all, words.

About the Author

Jennifer Probst is the author of *Write Naked*, *Write True*, and *Writers Inspiring Writers*. With more than fifty-five published novels across romance, women's fiction, and nonfiction, her books have been translated into multiple languages and sold millions of copies worldwide.

www.ingramcontent.com/pod-product-compliance
Lightning Source LLC
Chambersburg PA
CBHW031313160426
43196CB00007B/508